Mathematics for Computing

Mathematics for Computing

Rob Callan

Senior Lecturer
Systems Engineering Faculty, Southampton Institute

Letts Educational
Aldine Place
London W12 8AW
0181 740 2268

1998

A CIP catalogue record for this book is available from the British Library

ISBN 1–85805–375–7
Copyright Rob Callan © 1998

First edition 1998

Typeset by Tech Set Limited, Gateshead, Tyne & Wear.

Printed in Great Britain by
Ashford Colour Press, Gosport, Hants.

Contents

Preface

It is hardly surprising that college and university computing courses should attract many students hoping to develop careers as software professionals. Computing is interesting and there is hardly any aspect of our daily lives where a computer is not involved in one form or another from banking to the design of the cars we drive. At the time of writing there is a perceived shortage of skilled computing professionals. Those that have the necessary skills are in a strong bargaining position for salary and other perks. Also, there are some students who graduate and start on salaries in excess of those lecturers who have passed on their knowledge over the duration of study. The challenge though for the new graduate is to keep up to date with technology and for some there is the desire not to be just another typical computing professional but someone who can take new technology, assess its relevance, and push forward the frontiers of the profession.

Computers are machines that are built on mathematical principles and it is hardly surprising to find out that just about every aspect of computing is touched by mathematics. When you mention mathematics to many computing students their eyes glaze over, their head drops and they eagerly wait for the discussion to end; and yet these students desire to be systems analysts, designers, programmers and hopefully a combination of all three. A computer professional needs to be able to think logically and learn a new language whether that language is a programming language or a language that describes the design of a computer system. In fact the same skill set that is required for the study of mathematics. What might surprise many students is that they use mathematics all the time but the mathematics is not made explicit. You cannot program without an understanding of logic; you cannot even learn a programming language if you are not capable of learning the basic language of logic.

The aim of this book is to make explicit some of the mathematics that computing students and professionals use all the time. It provides a basic introduction and the material should be considered as a prerequisite to a computing degree. It is designed to be an introduction for students who are taking a first unit in 'computing mathematics' as part of a computing degree or HND. The author has a computing background, so the material is selected to be relevant to the needs of computing courses. The style will not suit those who like to see rigorous mathematical proofs – you will not find them here! Instead, I hope you will find an approachable introduction to many important topics that you can then pursue further, if necessary, with other books.

Much of the material in this book comes under the heading of discrete mathematics. The motivation for teaching discrete mathematics on many computing courses is to prepare the student for the study of formal methods. There are, though, plenty of reasons to study discrete maths, even if you are not motivated by the study of formal methods. A good understanding of basic logic will help you write better programs. Understanding relations and properties of relations is necessary for studying the object-oriented paradigm. Sets, logic and relations underpin the study of 'fuzzy systems'. Relations, sets, logic and linear algebra, etc., are required for the serious study of image processing, artificial intelligence, and neural networks – and so on. This book is an introduction and therefore some topics like algebraic structures, numerical methods and computational linguistics are not covered. Indeed, no book is likely to cover every topic.

The book is designed to be studied in sequence starting with Chapter 1 and ending with Chapter 9. It requires a basic general knowledge of mathematics; the level of mathematics you would have done at school. A few of the topics, however, require a more advanced knowledge of mathematics. It is typical for computing courses to provide a refresher unit in basic mathematics in recognition that many students may have returned to higher education having finished college some years earlier. If it is a while since you have used mathematics you might find the refresher course, *Refresher in Basic Mathematics* by P. N. Rowe (Letts Educational) of help. In general, the more difficult material is covered in Chapters 3 and 9. You might wish to delay the study of these chapters until other material is covered although the introductory material and applications in Chapter 3 should be manageable. You are encouraged to revisit chapters because a better understanding can sometimes be gleaned after meeting a topic again but in a different context.

When any subject is studied, it helps to be able to relate the theory to applications. Most topics conclude with a brief discussion of some areas of application. There are many application areas that are not mentioned to make the text more manageable for the reader, but the main purpose of these brief reviews is to try to convince the reader that the study of maths is important and that there is plenty to be gained once the mathematical skills have been acquired. Each chapter includes many examples and self-test questions that allow the reader to review a topic and check their understanding before progressing. Appendix A gives worked solutions to the self-test questions and Appendix B gives answers to the exercises. A bibliography recommends some other texts for those who wish to pursue their study beyond the introductory level.

1

Logic: Part I

Introduction

Most of us have some idea of what logic is even though we may struggle to give its definition. We often hear expressions like 'sounds logical' in response to a statement that somebody has made. That person might have been expressing their thoughts of how a puzzle could be solved. When we hear the solution, and if we understand and agree with the solution we might say, 'sounds logical'.

Logic is about reasoning and can be considered the backbone of computing. Computer programs are really a series of logical steps that solve a task.

It is widely recognised that many computer programs (if not most) contain bugs. A bug means that the program will not always behave as it was designed to. The word-processor package I am using to type this text sometimes decides to abandon the task and close with an error when I copy a picture. I am aware of the problem and usually can get around it, but it remains an irritation. Software bugs can be bad news. They can mean that a piece of software gets a bad reputation, sales are lost and a poor image of the company is created. The bug has more serious implications if the software is used in a safety-critical situation like air-traffic control. We need to be sure that such software is correct. We need to be sure that all of the software designers and programmers have understood what the software is supposed to do and we need to be sure that the work of the designers and programmers is correct. Logic can help us ensure that the whole software team (designers and programmers, etc.) have understood what the system should do and logic can help prove that the software is correct.

Members of a software team have to communicate their ideas and thoughts to other team members. Our standard and easiest way of communicating is to use language, either spoken or written. The problem with our everyday language is that the meaning of a statement is not always clear. For example, consider the following: suppose you are driving along a road and come to a toll bridge and there is a sign with charges and a notice 'make sure you have correct change'. What does this mean? Does it mean you should have the exact money in change so that traffic queues do not develop through having to wait? What if you don't, will you be turned away? Perhaps it means that you should check the money after the attendant gives you your change? The notice is ambiguous. Everyday English has to be used carefully to avoid ambiguous statements. It is difficult to be confident that ambiguity has been reduced even with careful use of everyday English because there are many ways of saying the

1

same thing and often there are many ways of interpreting the meaning of a statement. To reduce the chance of misinterpretation, our statements should be written using a language that restricts the way in which information can be expressed and each expression should have clear rules about how it should be interpreted. What we require then is a formal language. Logic is a formal language that can be used to make clear statements. Logic provides a language to represent information and to represent blocks of program code and for us to check that the code conforms to what the programmer intended.

This chapter looks at substituting symbols for sentences. Our intention is to learn a language that can be used in place of everyday natural language (like English). This language has rules just like English has rules about spelling and what makes a grammatical sentence. The language also has definitions for some of the symbols it uses. These definitions are given in the form of a truth table. We shall see what a truth table is and what the basic definitions of logic are. Finally we shall work our way towards doing proofs using logic. We shall extend our knowledge of logic in Chapter 3 before considering some applications of logic.

Symbols

A programming language restricts how lines of code can be written. For example, in the 'C' language if you want to test whether a variable is less than five you write:

```
if(x < 5)
```

The 'if' has to be written in lower-case letters and it has to be followed by an opening bracket. The 'C' language has a set of rules that define what is allowed. The line of 'C' code given above is an expression that is composed of symbols. All of the symbols like 'if' or '(' are recognised by the compiler. Our line of code uses correct syntax which means that it conforms to rules of the 'C' language. The following, for example, is not correct syntax:

```
If(x < 5)
```

because the 'i' in 'if' should be lower case. The 'C' language needs a set of rules so that the code can be interpreted and compiled into a program.

To communicate ideas using logic and to show a proof we need a language with a clear set of rules and definitions. The rules tell us what expressions can be written and the definitions tell us what the symbols of the language mean. The first step is to look at some basic definitions and to see how these definitions relate to everyday English.

Proposition

> A proposition is a statement that is either True or False. We shall use T to stand for true and F to stand for false.

An example proposition is:

>   Copper is a metal

This proposition is true and so has a value of T.

> If a proposition has a value T then it is a fact.

The statement:

>   Copper is not a metal

is also a proposition and has a value F because it is false. Another example is:

>   Five is less than six

which has a value T. The key thing to remember about propositions is that a **proposition can be assigned a value of true or false**. The sentence

>   How many miles is it from Southampton to Manchester?

is not a proposition. It makes no sense to say that this sentence is true or that it is false.

Propositions can be joined into what are known as compound propositions. An example is

>   John is seven and John likes pizza

which is composed of the proposition 'John is seven' and the proposition 'John likes pizza'. The propositions are joined with the word 'and'. This word is known as a 'connective' because it connects two propositions. Another commonly used connective is 'or'. Logic gives a precise definition to these connectives so that we can assign truth values to compound propositions. These definitions conform to our everyday notion of what 'and' and 'or' mean. For instance, the sentence

>   Sara plays rugby AND Sara plays tennis

is true provided 'Sara plays rugby' is true and provided that 'Sara plays tennis' is true. For the whole sentence (or compound proposition) to be true both component propositions must be true. If on the other hand we have

>   Sara plays rugby OR Sara plays tennis

the whole proposition is true provided that either 'Sara plays rugby' is true or 'Sara plays tennis' is true or both are true.

Example 1.1

Which of the following is a proposition?

(a) Copper is a metal.
(b) $5 < 3$
(c) What is the weather like?
(d) He likes pizza.

Solution
Sentence (a) is a proposition because it is true and sentence (b) is a proposition because it is false. Sentence (c) is not a proposition; it is a question and cannot be given a value true or false. Sentence (d) is not a proposition since 'He' is a variable and the person being referred to is not mentioned. How can you tell if that person likes pizza if that person is not identified?

Example 1.2

Which of the following compound propositions is true?

(a) $2 < 5$ AND $6 > 5$
(b) $2 < 5$ AND $6 > 8$
(c) $2 < 5$ OR $6 > 2$

Solution
Sentence (a) is true because both component propositions are true. Sentence (b) is false because '6 is greater than 8' is false. Sentence (c) is true because only one of the propositions need be true.

Truth tables and logical connectives

Truth tables are used to give the precise definitions for the logic connectives AND and OR. These connectives join two propositions and are known as binary connectives. It would be most inconvenient to write a separate truth table for every compound proposition that is encountered. To overcome this problem symbols are used in place of actual propositions. For example,

    A AND B

can be used to denote any two propositions connected by AND. The symbol A is a substitute for the first proposition and B is a substitute for the second. The symbols can be substitutes for any proposition. A single proposition like A or B is known as an atomic proposition. Since either symbol can have a value of T or F there are four possible combinations of truth values for A and B:

A is T, B is T

A is F, B is T

A is T, B is F

A is F, B is F

So, any compound proposition that has two component propositions has four possible interpretations; an interpretation is the assignment of T or F for a combination of the atomic propositions – it is a row in the truth table. For the AND connective, only one interpretation gives the value of T to the compound proposition; both atomic propositions need to be true. The truth table provides the concise definition:

A	B	A AND B
T	T	T
F	T	F
T	F	F
F	F	F

The truth table simply states that for 'A AND B' to have a value T then both A and B must have values T.

Logic connectives

Logic uses names and symbols to refer to the connectives. For example, AND is called conjunction and for shorthand notation uses the symbol $\wedge$. The names and symbols for the other connectives that will be of interest to us are given below.

Connective
$\wedge$ (AND) called conjunction.
$\vee$ (OR) called disjunction.
$\neg$ (NOT) called negation.
$\rightarrow$ (IMPLIES) also expressed as an if-then statement. Another term used is conditional.
$\leftrightarrow$ (EQUIVALENCE) called equivalence or sometimes double-implication.

AND

The truth table definition for AND was given earlier as

A	B	A ∧ B
T	T	T
F	T	F
T	F	F
F	F	F

OR

The definition for OR is

A	B	A ∨ B
T	T	T
F	T	T
T	F	T
F	F	F

NOT

Another very simple connective is NOT which has the definition

A	¬A
T	F
F	T

For example, we know that the proposition 'copper is a metal' is true and so if we say 'copper is NOT a metal' we get a value of false. The NOT connective is a unary connective because its definition applies to a single symbol.

Implication

Another important binary connective allows us to use logic to represent expressions of the form

If A THEN B

The 'If…then…' connective is called implication. Consider a horse race where Sara has placed money on a horse called Top-hat:

If Top-hat wins the race THEN Sara wins money

Let us consider the four possible interpretations for this proposition

1. Top-hat wins the race, Sara wins money   (T, T)
2. Top-hat wins the race, Sara does not win money   (T, F)
3. Top-hat does not win the race, Sara wins money   (F, T)
4. Top-hat does not win the race, Sara does not win money   (F, F)

The first thing to agree on is that the proposition only makes a statement about what happens if Top-hat wins; it says nothing about what will happen if Top-hat loses. The first of the four possibilities is consistent with the proposition since it says that Top-hat won and Sara won her money which is what we would expect. The second is inconsistent with the proposition since Sara should have won money because Top-hat won. The third and fourth are also consistent because the proposition tells us nothing of what happens if Top-hat loses: Sara might have placed a bet on another horse and still won money even though Top-hat lost or Sara might not have placed another bet in which case she will not have won any money.

   The definition of implication fits with the interpretation we have given to the possibilities of Top-hat's performance:

A	B	$A \rightarrow B$
T	T	T
F	T	T
T	F	F
F	F	T

Equivalence

The definition of equivalence is

A	B	$A \leftrightarrow B$
T	T	T
F	T	F
T	F	F
F	F	T

Equivalence is shorthand for $(A \rightarrow B) \wedge (B \rightarrow A)$ and is sometimes called double-implication. We can use a truth table to check that $A \leftrightarrow B$ is the same as $(A \rightarrow B) \wedge (B \rightarrow A)$. We construct a truth table with four rows because we have two symbols A and B.

1 A	2 B	3 $A \rightarrow B$	4 $B \rightarrow A$	5 $(A \rightarrow B) \wedge (B \rightarrow A)$
T	T	T	T	T
F	T	T	F	F
T	F	F	T	F
F	F	T	T	T

Columns 3 and 4 are just the component propositions that make up $(A \to B) \land (B \to A)$. Column 3 is the truth table definition for $(A \to B)$. The values in column 4 for $B \to A$ are easy to see from the definition of implication if we imagine columns 1 and 2 as being swapped. Column 5 is the AND of column 3 with column 4 and its truth values match with the definition of equivalence and so we have shown that $A \leftrightarrow B$ is the same as $(A \to B) \land (B \to A)$.

Example 1.3

Use a truth table to decide on the truth of the following sentences:

(a) London is the capital of the UK and Paris is the capital of France

(b) English is the native language of the UK and English is the native language of France

(c) French is the native language of the UK or French is the native language of France

(d) If Jupiter is a planet Then tennis is a sport

Solution
In both (a) and (b) the propositions are joined by AND. In (a) we let A denote 'London is the capital of the UK' and B denote 'Paris is the capital of France'. Both A is true and B is true and so looking in the truth table for 'A AND B' we see that 'A AND B' is true. In (b), B denotes 'English is the native language of France' which is false and so the combination is T for A and F for B. Therefore the answer for (b) is false. In (c) A is false, B is true and so we need to look up the combination 'F T' in the truth table for OR from which we see the answer is true. In (d) it is tempting to conclude that the sentence is false because it makes no sense but 'Jupiter is a planet' is true and 'tennis is a sport' is also true and therefore according to the definition of implication the sentence is true.

Equivalent logical expressions

Logical expressions can be re-written to an alternative form that has the same truth table interpretation; two expressions that have the same truth table interpretation are said to be equivalent. For example,

$\neg (A \lor B)$ is equivalent to $\neg A \land \neg B$

and can be proved using the truth table. The expression has two atomic symbols and so there are four rows in the truth table. We find the truth table values for the compound propositions either side of the equivalence and show that the columns of values are the same.

1 A	2 B	3 $\neg A$	4 $\neg B$	5 $\neg A \land \neg B$	6 $A \lor B$	7 $\neg (A \lor B)$
T	T	F	F	F	T	F
F	T	T	F	F	T	F
T	F	F	T	F	T	F
F	F	T	T	T	F	T

Columns 1 and 2 are the basic truth value combinations for two atomic symbols. Columns 5 and 7 are the compound expressions that we are attempting to show are equivalent. To work out the truth values for column 5 we first need to take the component expressions connected by AND and form columns 3 and 4. Columns 3 and 4 are computed from the basic truth table definition for NOT. The truth values for column 5 can then be computed by applying the definition for AND to columns 3 and 4. The expression in column 6 is extracted from the expression in column 7 and the truth values for column 6 are simply the truth table definition for OR ; column 7 follows by negating column 6.

The above table shows that the two shaded columns have the same truth values and therefore the two expressions are equivalent. Recognising equivalent expressions is useful when we wish to simplify expressions or to define one connective in terms of another.

Example 1.4

Show that $A \to B$ is logically equivalent to $\neg A \vee B$.

Solution
The truth table gives:

A	B	$A \to B$	$\neg A$	$\neg A \vee B$
T	T	T	F	T
F	T	T	T	T
T	F	F	F	F
F	F	T	T	T

Once again in this example we have broken down the expression into its simple components (i.e., atomic parts) and then combined them. In this way we build up the truth values for more complex expressions. Both shaded columns have the same truth values in the same order and so the expressions are equivalent.

Expressions with more than two atomic propositions

We have looked at the definitions for four binary connectives. In total there are sixteen binary connectives that can be defined. However, the main ones of interest to us are the four that have been introduced. Also, through equivalent expressions we can define all other binary connectives by rewriting them using the three connectives: AND, OR and IMPLICATION.

So far we have dealt with the truth for logical expressions of only two symbols. How do we handle expressions with three or more symbols? The answer is in the same way. The only real difference is the size of the truth table. With two atomic propositions we have 2^2 combinations of T and F. For three atomic propositions there are 2^3 or eight combinations and so the truth table has eight rows:

A	B	C
T	T	T
F	T	T
T	F	T
F	F	T
T	T	F
F	T	F
T	F	F
F	F	F

Example 1.5

Find the truth table for the expression $[P \lor (Q \land R)]$

Solution

P	Q	R	$Q \land R$	$P \lor (Q \land R)$
T	T	T	T	T
F	T	T	T	T
T	F	T	F	T
F	F	T	F	F
T	T	F	F	T
F	T	F	F	F
T	F	F	F	T
F	F	F	F	F

Use of brackets in logical expressions

We could define an order of precedence for our connectives just as we do for mathematical expressions. For example, if $\times$ has a higher precedence than $+$ we know that

$$3 + 2 \times 6$$

gives the value 15 instead of 30 because the multiply operation is done before the addition. In general it is clearer to write the expression using brackets like

$$3 + (2 \times 6)$$

to indicate the order of precedence. We adopt the same practice for logical expressions but it is still useful to define a precedence.

> The order of precedence is $\neg, \land, \lor, \rightarrow, \leftrightarrow$ which means that if there are no brackets then $\neg$ should be applied before $\land$ which should be applied before $\lor$ and so on. For example:
>
> $A \land B \rightarrow C$ is the same as $(A \land B) \rightarrow C$
> $A \land B \lor \neg C$ is the same as $(A \land B) \lor (\neg C)$
> $A \lor B \land C$ is the same as $A \lor (B \land C)$

Example 1.6

Show that $[P \vee (Q \wedge R)]$ is logically equivalent to $[(P \vee Q) \wedge (P \vee R)]$.

Solution

P	Q	R	$P \vee Q$	$P \vee R$	$[(P \vee Q) \wedge (P \vee R)]$
T	T	T	T	T	T
F	T	T	T	T	T
T	F	T	T	T	T
F	F	T	F	T	F
T	T	F	T	T	T
F	T	F	T	F	F
T	F	F	T	T	T
F	F	F	F	F	F

We see that the last column is the same as the last column of the truth table for the previous example. Therefore $[P \vee (Q \wedge R)]$ is equivalent to $[(P \vee Q) \wedge (P \vee R)]$.

Just as a point of interest, there is a technique for a more concise presentation of a truth table. In Example 1.6 we were saved the effort of evaluating some expressions because we made use of the work done in Example 1.5. If, though, we evaluated all expressions we would end up with a truth table with a large number of columns. The table below uses a more concise presentation.

P	Q	R	$[P \vee (Q \wedge R)]$		$\leftrightarrow$	$[(P \vee Q)$	$\wedge$	$(P \vee R)]$
T	T	T	T	T	T	T	T	T
T	F	T	T	F	T	T	T	T
F	T	T	T	T	T	T	T	T
F	F	T	F	F	T	F	F	T
T	T	F	T	F	T	T	T	T
T	F	F	T	F	T	T	T	T
F	T	F	F	F	T	T	F	F
F	F	F	F	F	T	F	F	F
1	1	1	3	2	4	2	3	2

The bottom row shows at what stage each column of truth values were written. Note that the columns for stage 3 give the truth value for $[P \vee (Q \wedge R)]$ and $[(P \vee Q) \wedge (P \vee R)]$. Stage 4 is the last column to be evaluated and is the truth-values for the columns at stage 3 connected by equivalence. The column at stage 4 has all rows set to true and the expression

$$[P \vee (Q \wedge R)] \leftrightarrow [(P \vee Q) \wedge (P \vee R)]$$

is called a tautology. We shall have more to say about tautologies later on in the chapter.

Procedure for finding the truth table

The procedure for finding the truth table for an expression can be given as a number of basic steps:

- Count the number of atomic propositions, n.
- Calculate the number of required rows from 2^n.
- Fill in the columns for each atom with T and F. Notice that the first column follows the sequence TFTF..., the second TTFFTTFF..., the third TTTTFFFF..., etc. So the successive Ts and Fs go in powers of 2.
- Form the other columns by breaking the expression into simple component parts. For instance if given

$$((A \wedge B \to C) \to (A \to (B \to C)))$$

we see that the middle implication has the expressions $((A \wedge B) \to C)$ and $(A \to (B \to C))$ either side and so we need columns for both of these expressions. Before computing the truth values for these columns we need to break down the expressions further for $A \wedge B$ and $B \to C$. The truth values for each column are then computed using the truth table definitions for the basic connectives.

?

1.1

Answers appear in Appendix A.

1 What is the truth value of the following statements:
(a) 5 is odd and 3 is odd
(b) 6 is even or 6 is odd
(c) $4 + 8 = 12 \wedge 3 - 1 = 2$
(d) $4 + 8 = 12 \vee 9 + 5 = 9$
(e) if 6 is odd then 6 is odd
(f) if 3 is even then 5 is not even
(g) if 4 is greater than 3 then 5 is less than 3
(h) $6 > 8 \to 6 > 2$

2 Translate the following logical expressions into English.

   A – today is Thursday   B – tomorrow is Friday

(a) $A \wedge B$
(b) $A \vee B$
(c) $A \to B$

3 Show that $\neg(A \wedge B)$ is equivalent to $\neg A \vee \neg B$.

4 Show that $(A \wedge B) \wedge C$ is equivalent to $A \wedge (B \wedge C)$.

5 Given that P is true and Q is false, what is the truth value for $(P \vee Q) \to P$.

Representing English sentences using logic

If we are to reason about English statements using logic then we need to know how to represent English statements using the language of logic. In this chapter we are dealing with propositional logic. Propositional logic allows us to represent English sentences as one or more propositions that are linked using the logic connectives.

The first step in representing an English sentence is to identify the atomic propositions, that is, the simple statements for which we can attach a value of true or false. If the sentence has more than one atomic proposition then we need to identify the appropriate connectives for joining the propositions together. To identify the appropriate connective we need to know in what way the connectives can be expressed in English. For AND and OR the task is usually easy since they often appear explicit in the text as 'and' and 'or'. The word 'but' also indicates an AND connective. For example,

> John switched on the kettle but John forgot to fill the kettle with water

can be expressed as

> John switched on the kettle AND John forgot to fill the kettle with water

The implication connective, $A \rightarrow B$, can be expressed in a number of ways in English:

> If A, then B
> A implies B
> A only if B
> B follows from A
> B is a necessary condition for A

The equivalence connective, $A \leftrightarrow B$, can also appear as

> A if and only if B

An expression containing 'if and only if' is making a strong statement. For example, barring an accident or breakdown, etc., the driving laws in the UK demand that we wait at a red traffic light but we are not allowed to wait if the light is on green. This rule could be expressed as:

> 'Stop at the traffic lights if and only if the light is red.'

Remember that equivalence is also known as double-implication. So if we see that a light is red we know that any car at the lights will have stopped and if we see that a car has stopped then we know that the light is red. Of course in the real world we might say that this assumption is correct most of the time but not all of the time since there might be an accident or someone might break the law. We cannot capture this type of scenario using propositional logic. Propositional logic does not handle shades of grey – either something is taken to be true or it is taken to be false.

Example 1.7

Express the following sentences in propositional logic.

1. John is tall and slim.
2. Sara is either a nurse or doctor.
3. The battery is flat only if the car will not start.
4. A flat battery implies that the car will not start.
5. If the battery is flat then the car will not start.
6. A win for the Reds follows from scoring more goals than the Blues.
7. John either won the money or the holiday but John did not win both.

Solution

1. This sentence can be rewritten as 'John is tall and John is slim.' Substituting A for 'John is tall' and B for 'John is slim' gives

    $A \wedge B$

2. Substituting A for 'Sara is a nurse' and B for 'Sara is a doctor' gives

    $A \vee B$

3. Substituting A for 'the battery is flat' and B 'for the car will not start' gives

    $A \rightarrow B$

4. Same as 3.
5. Same as 3.
6. Substituting A for 'the Reds win' and B for 'the Reds score more goals than the Blues' gives

    $B \rightarrow A$

7. Notice that 7 can be rewritten as
    John won the money or John won the holiday but John did not win the holiday and the money.

    Substituting A for 'John won the money' and B for 'John won the holiday' gives

    $(A \vee B) \wedge \neg (A \wedge B)$

The above expression can be simplified if we use a binary connective known as 'exclusive-or'. With exclusive-or we are saying that one or the other proposition is true but both cannot be true. The truth table for exclusive-or is

A	B	$B \otimes A$
T	T	F
F	T	T
T	F	T
F	F	F

We can test that $(A \lor B) \land \lnot (A \land B)$ is equivalent to exclusive-or by giving its truth table:

A	B	$B \lor A$	$A \land B$	$\lnot(A \land B)$	$(A \lor B) \land \lnot (A \land B)$
T	T	T	T	F	F
F	T	T	F	T	T
T	F	T	F	T	T
F	F	F	F	T	F

Tautology and contradiction

An expression that always has a value of T, no matter what the truth values of its atoms, is called a tautology. If an expression is a tautology, then each row in its truth table will have a value of T. The next section will show why a tautology is of interest. An example tautology is

$$A \lor \lnot A$$

Whatever the truth value of A, the above expression will always be true. A contradiction on the other hand will always be false. For example

$$A \land \lnot A$$

always has a value of false no matter what the truth value of A.

Example 1.8

Show that $A \land B \to A$ is a tautology.

Solution

A	B	$A \land B$	$A \land B \to A)$
T	T	T	T
F	T	F	T
T	F	F	T
F	F	F	T

1.2

Answers appear in Appendix A.

1 Let A, B, and C stand for the following statements:

  A: Bananas are sweet

  B: Bananas are fruit

  C: Apples are fruit

Represent the following statements using symbols. Tip: take care with the order of precedence.
(a) Bananas and apples are fruit
(b) Either bananas or apples are fruit
(c) If bananas are fruit then apples are fruit
(d) Bananas are sweet only if bananas are fruit

2 Which of the following are tautologies or contradictions?
(a) An apple is a fruit and an apple is not a fruit
(b) A bird is an animal or a bird is not an animal
(c) $((A \wedge B) \wedge C) \leftrightarrow (A \wedge (B \wedge C))$

Arguments and validity

An argument presents a conclusion as following logically from a set of assumptions. We shall use an example to explain these terms. Consider the following:

> John's keys are in the car or hung up in the office. John's keys are not in the car. Therefore John's keys are hung up in the office.

The above three sentences form an argument. The first two sentences present assumptions and the third sentence is a conclusion. The argument is making the claim that the conclusion follows from the assumptions, that is, given the first two sentences we should be able to state that 'John's keys are hung up in the office'. It is typical to write the argument in a form that makes clear the assumptions and the conclusion. So the above argument would be written:

> John's keys are in the car or hung up in the office. $\left.\right\}$ Assumptions
> John's keys are not in the car.

> Therefore John's keys are hung up in the office.   Conclusion

We can attach symbols to the above propositions using P for 'John's keys are in the car' and Q for 'John's keys are hung up in the office'.

$$P \vee Q$$
$$\frac{\neg P}{Q}$$

If an argument is valid, then whenever the assumptions are true, the conclusion is true. More formally we can express an argument as:

$$[A_1, A_2, ..., A_n] \models B$$

where all the As are assumptions and B is the conclusion. The symbol '$\models$' is called the semantic turnstile and is used to denote that the assumptions logically imply the conclusion. The expression indicates that whenever A_1, A_2, A_3 ... all have a value T, then B also has value T. For example, in the expression

$$P, P \rightarrow Q \models Q$$

when both P and $P \rightarrow Q$ are true then Q is true.

We shall soon see how to prove an argument valid using the rules of inference. First we shall see how to show that an argument is valid using a truth table. If we express the argument in the form

$$A_1 \wedge A_2 \wedge ... \wedge A_n] \rightarrow B$$

and show that the expression is a tautology then the argument is valid otherwise it is invalid. So returning to our example with John's keys we can present the argument as

$$((P \vee Q) \wedge \neg P) \rightarrow Q$$

Note that all we have done is simply to state that the conjunction of the assumptions implies the conclusion.

To see if the argument is valid we find its truth table:

P	Q	$P \vee Q$	$\neg P$	$(P \vee Q) \wedge \neg P$	$((P \vee Q) \wedge \neg P) \rightarrow Q$
T	T	T	F	F	T
F	T	T	T	T	T
T	F	T	F	F	T
F	F	F	T	F	T

According to the truth table $((P \vee Q) \wedge \neg P) \rightarrow Q$ is a tautology and therefore valid.

Example 1.9

Show that the following argument is valid.

> If John takes too long to calculate employees' salaries then the software is too slow but John takes too long to calculate the salaries therefore the software is too slow.

Solution
In the standard form the argument is presented as

> If John takes too long to calculate employees' salaries
> then the software is too slow.   } Assumptions
>
> John takes too long to calculate the salaries.
>
> The software is too slow.   Conclusion

P – John takes too long to calculate employees' salaries.
Q – the software is too slow.

$P \rightarrow Q$
P Assumptions

Q Conclusion

The expression that we need to show as a tautology is: $((P \rightarrow Q) \wedge P) \rightarrow Q$

P	Q	$P \rightarrow Q$	$(P \rightarrow Q) \wedge P$	$((P \rightarrow Q) \wedge P) \rightarrow Q$
T	T	T	T	T
F	T	T	F	T
T	F	F	F	T
F	F	T	F	T

The argument is a tautology and therefore is a valid argument.

Example 1.10

Show that the following argument is valid.

> If the interest rate increases then the mortgage rate increases. If the mortgage rate increases then house sales will fall. Either the interest rate will increase or the mortgage rate will increase therefore house sales will fall.

Solution
This example may appear a little more complicated than the previous example but we always follow the same procedure of breaking the argument down into its basic components and then construct the logical expression that represents the argument. The first thing to do is to identify the conclusion. The conclusion is the final statement that says 'house sales will fall'. The above argument is claiming that this conclusion follows from the previous statements. So the argument is:

If the interest rate increases then the mortgage rate increases.

If the mortgage rate increases then house sales will fall.

Either the interest rate will increase or the mortgage rate will increase.

Assumptions

House sales will fall.   Conclusion

P – interest rate increases.
Q – mortgage rate increases
R – house sales will fall

Using logic connectives we get

$$P \rightarrow Q$$

$$Q \rightarrow R$$

$$\frac{P \vee Q}{R}$$

The assumption and conclusions are now clearly identified. Taking the conjunction of the assumptions as implying the conclusion gives

$$((P \rightarrow Q) \wedge (Q \rightarrow R) \wedge (P \vee Q)) \rightarrow R$$

The next step is to compute the truth table for the above expression.

P	Q	R	a $P \rightarrow Q$	b $Q \rightarrow R$	c $P \vee Q$	d $a \wedge b$	e $d \wedge c$	$e \rightarrow R$
T	T	T	T	T	T	T	T	T
F	T	T	T	T	T	T	T	T
T	F	T	F	T	T	F	F	T
F	F	T	T	T	F	T	F	T
T	T	F	T	F	T	F	F	T
F	T	F	T	F	T	F	F	T
T	F	F	F	T	T	F	F	T
F	F	F	T	T	F	T	F	T

Note that the lower-case letters denote whole expressions. For example, a is a substitute for $P \rightarrow Q$ and is used for convenience. So the expression is a tautology and the argument therefore is valid.

Rules of inference

Truth tables provide a mechanical way of proving the validity of an argument. However, truth tables become cumbersome when there are many atomic propositions. For instance, if the argument has five atomic propositions then the truth table needs 2^5 (32) rows. An alternative to truth tables is to use what are known as 'rules of inference'. These rules enable us to spot whether the form of an expression is a tautology, and if it is, we can take the conclusion to be true from the assumption. For instance, in Example 1.9, the argument is of the form:

$$P \rightarrow Q, P \vdash Q \text{ or alternatively expressed as}$$

$$\left. \begin{array}{l} P \rightarrow Q \\ P \end{array} \right\} \text{Assumptions}$$

$$Q \qquad \text{Conclusion}$$

One of the rules of inference is known as modus-ponens and is defined as

$$A \rightarrow B$$

$$\frac{A}{\therefore B}$$

Modus-ponens states that if we accept the assumptions as true then we can conclude B (i.e., that B is true). Using this rule we could have spotted immediately that $P \rightarrow Q$, $P \models Q$ is a valid argument because apart from the choice of atomic symbols it has the same form as the modus-ponens rule. A list of some of the basic rules is given in Table 1.

Table 1

$\wedge$ elimination	$\dfrac{A \wedge B}{A}$ and $\dfrac{A \wedge B}{B}$
$\wedge$ introduction	$\dfrac{A, B}{A \wedge B}$
$\vee$ elimination	$\dfrac{A \rightarrow C, B \rightarrow C, A \vee B}{C}$
$\vee$ introduction	$\dfrac{A}{A \vee B}$ and $\dfrac{B}{A \vee B}$
Modus-ponens	$\dfrac{A, A \rightarrow B}{B}$
Double negation	$\dfrac{\neg \neg A}{A}$
Transitive	$A \rightarrow B$ $\dfrac{B \rightarrow C}{A \rightarrow C}$

The above rules are derived from their truth tables. For example, $\wedge$ introduction, states that if we assume both A and B (or are told that A is true and B is true) we can assume or conclude $A \wedge B$. The commas in the above table separate the logical expressions that we are assuming to be true in order to state the conclusion. So for $\vee$ elimination, if we know that $A \rightarrow C$ is true and $B \rightarrow C$ is true and $A \vee B$ is true we can conclude C.

We can use the above rules to show that an argument is valid. The argument is laid out in a series of steps. A step might simply involve writing an assumption or it could be a simplification of an expression using an elimination rule or the construction of an expression using an introduction rule. Eventually we should reach a step which shows the conclusion as following from the assumptions. A step can also be a tautology. For example, we may already know from previously constructing a truth table that a simple expression is a tautology.

Example 1.11

Show that the following argument is valid.

$$(P \wedge Q)$$
$$\frac{(P \vee Q) \to R}{R}$$

Solution

1. $(P \wedge Q)$ assumption
2. $(P \vee Q) \to R$ assumption
3. P using 1 and $\wedge$ elimination
4. $(P \vee Q)$ using 3 and $\vee$ introduction
5. R using 2, 4 and modus-ponens

Steps 1 and 2 simply list the assumptions. Step 3 applies a rule to the assumption listed as step 1, and step 4 is the result of applying a rule to step 3. Finally, using modus-ponens we conclude R and so the argument is valid.

Example 1.12

Show that the following argument is valid.

$$(P \to Q)$$
$$(Q \to R)$$
$$\frac{P}{R}$$

Solution

1. $(P \to Q)$ assumption
2. $(Q \to R)$ assumption
3. $(P \to R)$ transitive rule and using 1 and 2.
4. P assumption
5. R modus-ponens on 3 and 4

?   **1.3**

Answers appear in Appendix A.

1 Use a truth table to show that the following arguments are valid

(a) $P \to Q$
        $\dfrac{Q \vee P}{Q}$

(b) P

       Q

      $\dfrac{(P \wedge Q) \rightarrow R}{R}$

2 Repeat Question 1 using the rules of inference.

Summary

- A proposition is a statement that is either True or False. If a proposition has a value T then it is a fact.
- Binary connectives

A	B	$A \wedge B$	$A \vee B$	$A \rightarrow B$	$A \leftrightarrow B$
T	T	T	T	T	T
F	T	F	T	T	F
T	F	F	T	F	F
F	F	F	F	T	T

- Two logical expressions can be shown to be equivalent by showing that their truth tables are the same.
- An expression that always has a value of T, no matter what the truth values of its atoms, is called a tautology. A contradiction on the other hand will always be false.
- An argument presents a conclusion as following logically from a set of assumptions.
- Rules of inference:

$\wedge$ elimination	$\dfrac{A \wedge B}{A}$ and $\dfrac{A \wedge B}{B}$
$\wedge$ introduction	$\dfrac{A, B}{A \wedge B}$
$\vee$ elimination	$\dfrac{A \rightarrow C, B \rightarrow C, A \vee B}{C}$
$\vee$ introduction	$\dfrac{A}{A \vee B}$ and $\dfrac{B}{A \vee B}$
Modus-ponens	$\dfrac{A, A \rightarrow B}{B}$
Double negation	$\dfrac{\neg \neg A}{A}$
Transitive	$A \rightarrow B$ $B \rightarrow C$ $A \rightarrow C$

EXERCISES

Answers appear in Appendix B.

1 Which of the following are propositions?
   (a) A dog is a type of animal
   (b) He likes cats
   (c) $5 < 2$
   (d) Is tomorrow Wednesday?

2 Give the truth value for each of the following:
   (a) London is a city
   (b) $6 > 8$
   (c) $6 > 8 \vee 5 < 2$
   (d) A cube has six sides and eight corners
   (e) $(4 < 6) \rightarrow (8 > 12)$
   (f) $(4 < 6) \rightarrow (8 > 2)$
   (g) (4 is even) $\vee$ (3 is odd)
   (h) ((4 is even) $\vee$ (3 is odd)) $\rightarrow$ 7 is odd

3 Give the truth table for each of the following expressions:
   (a) $\neg(P \rightarrow Q)$
   (b) $P \wedge \neg Q$
   (c) $P \wedge P$
   (d) $\neg(P \rightarrow \neg Q)$
   (e) $\neg P \rightarrow Q$
   (f) $(P \vee Q) \wedge (P \vee R)$
   (g) $(P \rightarrow Q) \rightarrow R$
   (h) $P \rightarrow (P \vee R)$

4 Use a truth table to show that
   (a) $P \vee (Q \wedge R)$ is equivalent to $(P \vee Q) \wedge (P \vee R)$
   (b) $P \wedge Q$ is equivalent to $\neg(\neg P \vee \neg Q)$
   (c) $P \wedge Q$ is equivalent to $\neg(P \rightarrow \neg Q)$

5 Let A, B, and C stand for the following statements:
   A: A plane flies (or can fly)
   B: A plane uses fuel
   C: A plane is expensive

   Translate the following into symbolic notation.
   (a) A plane can fly and a plane uses fuel
   (b) If a plane flies then a plane uses fuel
   (c) If a plane flies and a plane uses fuel then a plane is expensive
   (d) A plane flies only if it uses fuel

6 Let A, B, and C stand for the following statements:
   A: John drinks tea
   B: John drinks coffee
   C: John drinks milk

Translate the following into English.

(a) $A \lor \neg A$

(b) $A \to C$

(c) $(A \lor B) \to C$

(d) $A \to \neg B$

7 Use a truth table to prove

$\neg \neg P$

$P \to Q$

$\dfrac{P \land Q \to R}{R}$

8 Use a truth table to prove

Q

$P \lor Q \to R$

$\dfrac{R \to P}{P}$

9 Repeat Exercise 7 using the rules of inference.

10 Repeat Exercise 8 using the rules of inference.

11 Show that the following argument is valid:

If David takes the maths lecture then the class finishes early. If the class finishes early David can get to the match. David takes the maths lecture. Therefore David can get to the match.

2

Sets

Introduction

Many concepts in computing are expressed using set notation and so sets form a fundamental topic; in fact set theory is used to describe the majority of mathematical topics. The main role of this chapter is to ensure that you are familiar with the language of sets, as it is a prerequisite for subsequent chapters.

What is a set?

A set is a collection of objects that share some property. For example, all of the players in a football team can be placed in a set and the defining property is that each member of the set plays for that particular team.

A capital letter is used to denote a set and the members of a set are listed inside braces {}. If an object x is a member of a set A then we write

$x \in A$ x belongs to A.

If x is not a member of A we write

$x \notin A$ x does not belong to A.

Example 2.1

For the sets A and B which of the following statements is true:

$A = \{2, 3, 6, 7\}$

$B = \{\text{orange, red, blue, green}\}$

1. $6 \in A$
2. $7 \in A$
3. $5 \in A$
4. $5 \notin A$
5. *blue* $\in B$
6. *blue* $\notin B$

Solution

1. True, since 6 is a member of A.

2. True.

3. False, 5 is not a member of A.

4. True, because 5 is not a member of A.

5. True.

6. False.

Two sets are equal if and only if they contain the same elements. The order of elements in a set does not matter. Also, each element is listed only once. If the sets A and B are equal we write

$A = B$

And if they are not equal we write

$A \neq B$

Example 2.2

Which of the following sets is equal to $\{6, 7, 8\}$

1. $\{6, 7, 8\}$
2. $\{7, 6, 8\}$
3. $\{7, 8\}$
4. $\{8, 7, 6\}$

Solution

All sets apart from $\{7, 8\}$ are equal to $\{6, 7, 8\}$. The set $\{7, 8\}$ is not equal to $\{6, 7, 8\}$ because the element 6 is missing.

Defining the members of a set

One way of defining the members of a set is to list the elements but for large sets this is inconvenient. Another way to define the members of a set is to use the notation

$\{x \mid P(x)\}$ the set of all x such that x has property P.

The property $P(x)$ is also known as a predicate and may be described using a simple English statement or may be described using mathematical notation.

Example 2.3

List the elements of the following sets

1. $\{x \mid x$ is an integer that is greater than 0 and less than 10$\}$
2. $\{x \mid x$ is an integer and $0 < x < 10\}$
3. $\{x \mid x = 2y$ and $y \in \{1, 2, 4, 6\}\}$

Solution

1. $\{1, 2, 3, 4, 5, 6, 7, 8, 9\}$
2. Same set as in Question 1 but the property is expressed using a different notation.
3. $\{2, 4, 8, 12\}$. The property states that each member x is twice the value of y. The members of y are listed.

2.1

Answers appear in Appendix A.

1 Which of the following is true?
  (a) $\{2, 3, 4, 5\} = \{5, 4, 3, 2\}$
  (b) $\{5, 6, 7, 8\} = \{6, 7, 8\}$
  (c) $6 \in \{5, 6, 7, 9\}$
  (d) $8 \in \{5, 6, 7, 9\}$

2 List the elements of the following sets
  (a) $\{x \mid x$ is an integer with $5 \leq x < 8\}$
  (b) $\{x \mid x = y$ and $y \in \{5, 6, 8\}\}$
  (c) $\{x \mid x = z^3$ and $z \in \{-2, -1, 0, 1, 2\}\}$

Sets within sets

A set may contain other sets as members. For example,

$$A = \{\{1, 2\}, \{4, 5\}, \{7, 8\}\}$$

The set A has three members and each member is a set. It is important to realise that

$$\{\{1\}, \{2\}, \{3\}\} \neq \{1, 2, 3\}$$

since both sets have different members: one has sets as members and the other has integers.

The empty or null set contains no elements and is written as $\{\}$. The symbol $\varnothing$ is also used to denote the empty set.

Some standard sets

There are some sets that are referred to so frequently that it is convenient to use characters to denote these sets.

N = the set of all natural numbers (i.e., 0 and positive integers).
Z = the set of all integers
R = the set of all real numbers (e.g., 3.45, −8.96, etc.)

Note that we could also write

N = {0, 1, 2, 3, ...}
Z = {...−3, −2, −1, 0, 1, 2, 3...}

We can define the sets in this manner because it should be clear what the pattern is, in other words, we can list other elements in the set by noting how the elements progress in sequence.

Relations between sets

The equal relationship has already been introduced. Another relationship is subset (and proper subset).

> A set A is a subset of a set B if every member of A is also a member of B. For example,
>
> $A = \{3, 4, 6\}$
> $B = \{5, 6, 9, 4, 2, 3\}$
>
> A is a subset of B. The relationship A is a subset of B is written as
>
> $A \subseteq B$

Note that we can also express the subset relationship more formally using the language introduced in Chapter 1:

$$A \subseteq B \leftrightarrow (\forall x, x \in A \rightarrow x \in B)$$

The symbol $\forall x$ will be introduced in Chapter 3 but it means 'for all values of x'.

This formal definition is presented to illustrate how mathematics can be used to give a concise formal definition – the formal aspect reduces the chance of misinterpretation.

A set A is said to be a proper subset of B if A is a subset of B but A is not equal to B (so B must contain an element that is not in A). The notation

$$A \subset B$$

denotes that A is a proper subset of B.

Every set has the empty set and itself as subsets

Example 2.4

Let

$A = \{5, 7, 8, 9\}$
$B = \{5, 8\}$
$C = \{5, 7, 8, 16\}$

Which of the following is true?

1. $B \subset A$
2. $B \subseteq A$
3. $B \subset C$
4. $C \notin A$
5. $\{5, 8, 16\} \subset C$
6. $\varnothing \subset A$

Solution

All of the above statements are true.

Example 2.5

Let

$A = \{x \mid x \in \mathsf{N} \text{ and } 10 < x \leq 20\}$
$B = \{11, 16, 20\}$
$C = \{x \mid x \in \mathsf{Z}\}$
$D = \{11, 12, 13, 14, 15, 16, 17, 18, 19, 20\}$

Which of the following is true?

1. $B \subset A$
2. $B \subseteq A$
3. $A \subset D$
4. $A \subseteq D$

5. $D \subseteq A$

6. $12 \in A$

7. $12 \subseteq A$

8. $\{12\} \subseteq A$

9. $B \subseteq C$

10. $\{12\} \in D$

Solution
Note that $A = D$ (they have the same members).

1. True

2. True

3. False because D has no element that is not a member of A.

4. True

5. True

6. True

7. False – 12 is not a set

8. True

9. True

10. False – D does not have any sets as members.

? **2.2**

Answers appear in Appendix A.

1 Let

        $A = \{$apple, orange, grape, banana, peach$\}$

        $B = \{$orange, grape, plum$\}$

        $C = \{$ apple, banana$\}$

Which of the following is true?

(a) $B \subset A$

(b) $B \subseteq A$

(c) $C \subset A$

(d) apple $\in C$

2 Which of the following is true?

(a) $\{-1, 2, 3\} \subset \mathsf{N}$

(b) $\{2, 3\} \subset \mathsf{Z}$

(c) $\{6, 8, 9\} \subset \mathsf{N}$

Operations on sets

An operation on a set produces another set or a number. An operation that works with a single set is a unary operation and an operation that works with two sets is a binary operation.

> The cardinality of a set is the number of elements in the set.

Example 2.6

Give the cardinality of the following sets

1. $\{3, 45, 6, 9\}$
2. $\{-1, -4, 9, 10, 11, 12\}$
3. {orange, blue}
4. {}
5. {0}

Solution

1. 4
2. 6
3. 2
4. 0
5. 1

> The power set of a set A, denoted PA, is the set of all subsets of A.

To find the power set for a set, we list all the subsets and then enclose these subsets within {} to form the power set. We need to remember that a set has itself as a subset and the empty set.

Example 2.7

Give PA where

$$A = \{1, 4, 6\}$$

Solution
The subsets are

$$\{\}, \{1\}, \{4\}, \{6\}, \{1, 4\}, \{1, 6\}, \{4, 6\}, \{1, 4, 6\}$$

and so

$$PA = \{\{\}, \{1\}, \{4\}, \{6\}, \{1, 4\}, \{1, 6\}, \{4, 6\}, \{1, 4, 6\}\}$$

The number of elements in the power set is 2^n where n is the number of elements in A.

> The union of two sets is a set that combines the elements of the two sets. The union of sets A and B is written
>
> $$A \cup B$$

If we have

$$C = A \cup B$$

then every member of C is either a member of A or a member of B (more formally

$$C = \{x \mid x \in A \text{ or } x \in B\}).$$

If $A = \{3, 4, 6\}$ and $B = \{8, 9, 4\}$ then the union is $\{3, 4, 6, 8, 9\}$. Although 4 appears in both sets it is listed only once in the union (remember that members are not repeated).

> The intersection of two sets is a set that contains elements that appear in both sets. So the intersection of A and B is written,
>
> $$A \cap B$$
>
> will be a set whose elements appear both in A and B.

If $A = \{3, 4, 6\}$ and $B = \{8, 9, 4\}$ then $A \cap B = \{4\}$

> The difference between two sets A and B, written $A - B$ (or as $A \backslash B$) is a set whose elements belong to A but do not belong to B. If $A = \{3, 4, 6\}$ and $B = \{8, 9, 4\}$ then
>
> $$A - B = \{3, 6\}$$

To find the difference we start with a set, say C, that is equal to A and then we inspect each element of B and if that element appears in A we eliminate it from C. So, to find $B - A$ using the sets in the above example we shall form a set C that is equal to B,

$$C = \{8, 9, 4\}$$

We now inspect each element of A and see if it appears in C. The element 3 does not appear in C but 4 does and so we remove it

$$C = \{8, 9\}$$

The final element of A is 6 and does not appear in C and so

$$B - A = \{8, 9\}$$

The universal set and complement

For a particular problem, it is often useful to define what is known as a 'universal set' for which all other sets are subsets of. If we denote the universal set by U and we have

$$U = N$$

Then $\{2, 3, 6, 7\}$ and $\{9, 10, 30, 89\}$ are subsets of U.

The complement of a set A, written A^c, is the set of elements that belong to U but not to A. For example, if

$$U = \{1, 2, 3, 4, 5, 6, 7, 8, 9\}$$
and $\quad A = \{1, 2, 3, 4, 6, 8\}$

then

$$A^c = \{5, 7, 9\}$$

Example 2.8

Let

$$U = \{1, 2, 3, 4, 5, 6, 7, 8, 9, 21, 22, 23, 24, 25, 26\}$$
$$A = \{1, 2, 3, 8, 9\}$$
$$B = \{8, 1, 3, 25, 26\}$$
$$C = \{8, 25, 26, 4\}$$

Find
1. $A \cup B$
2. $A \cap B$
3. $A - B$
4. A^c
5. $(A \cap B) \cap C$

Solution
1. $A \cup B = \{1, 2, 3, 8, 9, 25, 26\}$
2. $A \cap B = \{1, 3, 8\}$
3. $A - B = \{2, 9\}$
4. $A^c = \{4, 5, 6, 7, 21, 22, 23, 24, 25, 26\}$
5. $(A \cap B) \cap C = \{8\}$

Venn diagrams

Set operations can be represented using a Venn diagram (see Figure 2.1).

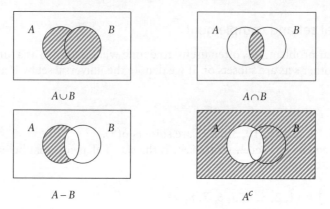

Figure 2.1   Diagram illustration of basic set operations.

?

2.3

Answers appear in Appendix A.

1 Let

$U = \{$Carl, John, David, Sara, Debbie, Sheila, Janet$\}$

$A = \{$Carl, John, David$\}$

$B = \{$David, Sara, Debbie$\}$

Find

(a) $A \cup B$

(b) $A \cap B$

(c) $A - B$

(d) $(A \cup B)^c$

(e) the cardinality of B

(f) $\mathbb{P}A$

Ordered pairs and cartesian product

The order of elements within a set does not matter. An ordered pair consists of two objects listed inside parentheses ( ) and the order of elements matters. For example, the sets $\{1, 2\}$ and $\{2, 1\}$ are equivalent but the pairs $(1, 2)$ and $(2, 1)$ are different.

There are many occasions where the ordering of objects is important. For example, the arithmetic operation of subtracting two integers produces a result that is dependent on the order in which the objects are taken:

$$1 - 2 = -1$$

whereas

$$2 - 1 = 1.$$

Now we know what an ordered pair is, we can define the cartesian product.

> The cartesian product of two sets A and B, written $A \times B$, is the set of all ordered pairs where the first object comes from A and the second from B.

The procedure for obtaining the cartesian product of A and B requires that each element of A be written as an ordered pair with every element of B. For example, let

$A = \{3, 4, 6\}$ and $B = \{8, 9, 4\}$ then

$A \times B = \{(3, 8), (3, 9), (3, 4), (4, 8), (4, 9), (4, 4), (6, 8), (6, 9), (6, 4)\}$

Example 2.9

Let

$A = \{1, 8\}$

$B = \{3, 4\}$

Find:

1. $A \times B$
2. $B \times A$
3. $A \times A$
4. $A \times A \times A$

Solution

1. $A \times B = \{(1, 3), (1, 4), (8, 3), (8, 4)\}$
2. $B \times A = \{(3, 1), (3, 8), (4, 1), (4, 8)\}$
3. $A \times A = \{(1, 1), (1, 8), (8, 1), (8, 8)\}$
4. $A \times A \times A = \{(1, 1, 1), (1, 1, 8), (1, 8, 1), (1, 8, 8), (8, 1, 1), (8, 1, 8), (8, 8, 1), (8, 8, 8)\}$

Note that for 4, we have taken the pairs for 3 and combined with each element in A to create what is known as a set of triples (three objects).

Summary

- A set is a collection of objects that share some property. A capital letter is used to denote a set and the members of a set are listed inside braces {}. We write:

  $x \in A$ x belongs to A.

  $x \notin A$ x does not belong to A.

- Two sets are equal if and only if they contain the same elements. Another way to define the members of a set is to use the notation

  $\{x \mid P(x)\}$ the set of all x such that x has property P.

- A set A is a subset of a set B if every member of A is also a member of B. A set A is said to be a proper subset of B if A is a subset of B but A is not equal to B.
- The cardinality of a set is the number of elements in the set.
- The power set of a set A, denoted $\mathbb{P}A$, is the set of all subsets of A and will include the empty set and itself as members.
- The union of two sets is a set that combines the elements of the two sets. The union of sets A and B is written $A \cup B$.
- The intersection of two sets is a set that contains elements that appear in both sets. The intersection of A and B is written $A \cap B$.
- The difference between two sets A and B, written $A - B$ (or as $A\backslash B$) is a set whose elements belong to A but do not belong to B.
- The universal set $\mathbb{U}$ contains all the objects for the problem we are interested in. The complement of a set A, written A^c, is the set of elements that belong to $\mathbb{U}$ but not to A.
- An ordered pair consists of two objects listed inside parentheses ( ) and the order of elements matters. The cartesian product of two sets A and B, written $A \times B$, is the set of all ordered pairs where the first object comes from A and the second from B.

EXERCISES

Answers appear in Appendix B.

1 Which of the following is true?
   (a) $\{4, 5, 8\} = \{5, 8, 4\}$
   (b) $\{apple, orange\} = \{orange, apple\}$
   (c) $4 \in \{9, 5, 4, 6\}$
   (d) $\{\{4\}, 5\} = \{4, 5\}$
   (e) $6 \notin \{9, 5, 4, 6\}$
   (f) $\{3, 2\} \in \{\{0\}, \{1, 6, 5\}, \{2, 3\}\}$

2 Which of the following is true?
   (a) $\{2, 3, 4\} \subseteq \{2, 3, 4\}$
   (b) $\{2, 3\} \subseteq \{2, 3, 4\}$
   (c) $\{2, 3\} \subset \{2, 3, 4\}$
   (d) $\{5\} \subseteq \{\{4\}, \{6\}, \{5\}\}$
   (e) $\{\} \subset \{2, 3, 4\}$

3 List the elements of the following sets
   (a) $\{x\,|\,x$ is an integer with $-2 < x < 4\}$
   (b) $\{x\,|\,x \in N$ and $x < 10\}$
   (c) $\{x\,|\,x = y$ and $y \in \{6, 7, 9\}\}$
   (d) $\{x\,|\,x$ is a capital city in Europe and $x \in \{$Paris, Washington$\}\}$

4 Give the cardinality of the following sets
   (a) $\{3, 4, 8\}$
   (b) $\{6, 10, 11, 12\}$
   (c) $\{10, \{4, 5, 6\}\}$
   (d) $\{\{\ \}, 10, \{12, \{11\}\}\}$

5 Evaluate the following
   (a) $\mathrm{P}\{2\}$
   (b) $\mathrm{P}\{10, 11, 18\}$
   (c) $\mathrm{P}\,\mathrm{P}\,\{2\}$

6 Evaluate the following
   (a) $\{3, 4, 9\} \cup \{5, 8, 11\}$
   (b) $\{3, 4, 9\} \cup \{5, 8, 9\}$
   (c) $\{3, 4, 9\} \cap \{5, 8, 9\}$
   (d) $\{$red, green, blue$\} \cap \{$blue, yellow$\}$
   (e) $\{\{9\}, 4, 5\} \cap \{9, 4, 5\}$
   (f) $(\{1, 2, 3\} \cap \{3, 5, 6, 2\}) \cap (\,\{3, 8\}$
   (g) $\{3, 8\} \cap (\{1, 2, 3\} \cap \{3, 5, 6, 2\})$

7 Let
   $U = \{-16, -15, -14, -12, 5, 8, 10, 12, 14, 20\}$
   $A = \{-12, -16, 5, 10, 12\}$
   $B = \{8, 14, 10, 5\}$

   Evaluate
   (a) $A \cap B$
   (b) $A - B$
   (c) $B - A$
   (d) $(A - B) \cap B$
   (e) A^c
   (f) B^c

8 Let
   $A = \{3, 4\}$
   $B = \{6, 8, 2\}$

   Evaluate
   (a) $A \times B$
   (b) $B \times A$
   (c) $A \times A$

3

Logic: Part II

Introduction

In Chapter 1 we were concerned with propositional logic. Propositional logic, although very useful, is limited in its expressiveness. For instance, suppose we wished to represent the following using logic notation:

> John loves Mary
>
> Sara loves David
>
> Debbie loves Rob

Using propositional logic, each statement is given its own atomic symbol like A. If we symbolise each statement as A, B and C, we no longer represent the similarity that each statement shares. The similarity is that each statement has a common relationship 'love'. This is one reason why we say that propositional logic is limited in its expressive power. Consider another sentence,

> The girl that John loves is David's sister

If we represent this sentence using a single atomic symbol then we lose a lot of information. We have the relationships *love* and *sister* and the sentence also tells us that there is an indirect link between John and David.

'Predicate' logic is a more expressive logic than propositional logic. Predicate logic allows us to represent objects (e.g., David and John) and the relationships between objects. Predicate logic still uses the inference rules that were introduced in Chapter 1 and so we are not starting from scratch. Predicate logic also provides a way of reasoning about statements that could not be reasoned with using propositional logic. For example,

> Every person has a date of birth ⎫
>   ⎬ Assumptions
> John is a person   ⎭
>
> John has a date of birth   Conclusion

Although we can see that the conclusion would appear to be valid, we cannot show that it is using propositional logic but we can if we use predicate logic.

This chapter introduces the basics of predicate logic. Transforming English sentences into predicate symbols is harder than for propositional logic and so you should not be frustrated if you struggle more with some of the ideas. Showing the validity of arguments in predicate notation is also introduced but this is merely for illustration; there is no aim to equip the reader with skills to validate arguments expressed in predicate notation. The validating of predicate expressions relies on the inference rules from Chapter 1 with three new additional rules.

Predicate logic

Relations and objects

Consider the following passage:

> Misty is a horse. Teg is a horse. Friday is a horse. John owns Misty, Teg and Friday. Teg is a racehorse and Teg has won the gold cup.

The set of objects in the passage is

> {Misty, Teg, Friday, John}

and the set of relationships:

> {horse, racehorse, owns, won}

When objects are actually named, each member in the set of names is called a constant. Also, each member of the set of named relationships is called a predicate. You might feel unsure about how to identify objects and relations. To some extent it comes with practice. Objects are usually not that difficult to identify. An object is literally a 'thing'. For our purpose, an object is anything we could point to as a physical existing thing: a book, page, word, bike, soup, flower, car, etc. A predicate is a relation that involves one or more objects. A predicate has arguments, which are the objects that the relationship applies to. The term argument used here has a distinct meaning from that used in 'logical arguments' in Chapter 1: the term used here is more typically called parameter in computing. For instance, 'John loves Mary' can be written in predicate notation as

> loves(John, Mary).

The predicate is love and the arguments are *John* and *Mary*. The number of arguments that a predicate has is known as the 'arity'. For example, the predicate *love* has arity 2. Predicate names are written as starting with a lower-case character and constants as starting with an upper-case character.

Returning to our passage, how do we write 'Misty is a horse'. The sentence has a single object *Misty* and a single relationship *horse* and so the predicate form is:

horse(Misty).

Notice that we could have written the predicate as *is-a-horse*. The actual name used for the predicate is one of personal choice, the main requirement being that the name should clearly identify the relationship. Also once a name is adopted we should be consistent in its use. For example it is not acceptable to use *horse* in one instance and *is a horse* in another.

The complete passage:

Misty is a horse. Teg is a horse. Friday is a horse. John owns Misty, Teg and Friday. Teg is a racehorse and Teg has won the gold cup.

Can be represented as:

horse(Misty).
horse(Teg).
horse(Friday).
owns(John, Misty).
owns(John, Teg).
owns(John, Friday).
racehorse(Teg).
won(Teg, Gold-cup).

We have split the last sentence into two but we can use the logic connectives presented in Chapter 1. So the last sentence would be represented as:

racehorse(Teg) $\land$ won(Teg, Gold-cup).

Example 3.1

Represent the following sentences in predicate notation.

1. David is a boy and David loves Sara.
2. Sara is either a nurse or a doctor.
3. Anne is not a nurse.
4. If Misty is horse, and John owns Misty, then Misty is a racehorse.

Solution

1. boy(David) $\land$ loves(David, Sara).
2. nurse(Sara) $\lor$ doctor(Sara).
3. $\lnot$ nurse(Anne).
4. (horse(Misty) $\land$ owns(John, Misty)) $\rightarrow$ racehorse(Misty).

There is another type of relationship known as a functional relation or function. A function relates one object to exactly one other object. For example, *motherOf* is a functional relation since everyone has only one natural mother. So we could express

> Sara's mother is married to Alan

as

> married(motherOf(Sara), Alan).

Note that motherOf(Sara) gives another object who is Sara's mother. Functions can also be applied repeatedly. For instance

> motherOf(motherOf(Sara))

refers to Sara's grandmother.

The assignment of truth to predicate sentences

An atomic sentence in predicate logic is a predicate followed by parentheses, '( )', with one or more arguments. For example,

> brother(John, David)

or, as a more complex example

> married(motherOf(Sara), Alan).

We need to be able to assign a truth value to predicates just as we did with propositions in Chapter 1. Our notion of truth is quite intuitive. For instance,

> brother(John, David)

is true provided the *John* who is being referred to is the brother of *David* who is being referred to. We say that

> an atomic sentence is true provided that the relationship holds between the objects referred to by the arguments.

Although the notion of truth is quite intuitive we need to be a little more formal. One of the potential dangers of symbols is that they can be used in a rather arbitrary way. For instance, suppose we are looking at objects in a shipyard and *John* is a sailor but *David* is the name of a ship. So *John* belongs to the set of 'sailors' and *David* to the set of 'ships'. We might therefore be able to assign a value of true to

> on-board(John, David)

but not

    ship-mates(John, David)

because ship-mates is a relationship that applies to the set of sailors and *David* is not a sailor (of course if we had a sailor called David we could simply name one or other objects differently, e.g., ShipDavid).

    With predicate logic, when we assign a truth value, we have to be concerned with what is known as the 'domain of interpretation'. A domain is a non-empty set of objects.

    When we assign names to objects we are mapping (associating) the names to objects. For instance, Teg, Friday and Misty are real horses (i.e., objects) and we have mapped these names to those real horses. All the horses belong to the domain of objects we are dealing with. The symbol, $\mapsto$, is used to denote a mapping. Suppose the horses have labels (e.g., are branded as) horse_1, horse_2 and horse_3, then our mapping of names to horses could be expressed as

    Teg $\mapsto$ horse_1

    Friday $\mapsto$ horse_2

    Misty $\mapsto$ horse_3

All we have done with the mapping is to assign names to specified objects. You can think of the mapping simply as giving names to three horses. We also need to map relationship names to relationships over the domain. For example,

    horse $\mapsto$ {horse_1, horse_2, horse_3}

states that the horse_1, horse_2 and horse_3 are horses. Suppose for John we have

    John $\mapsto$ person_1

Now we can define the mapping for owns:

    owns $\mapsto$ {(person_1, horse_1), (person_1, horse_2), (person_1, horse_3)}

The *owns* relation is represented here as a set of ordered pairs. Since for our example

    person_1 = {John}

    horse_1 = Teg, horse_2 = Friday, horse_3 = Misty

we have

    {(John, Teg), (John, Friday), (John, Misty)}

representing the relation *owns*.

The interpretation of an atomic sentence is simply a case of looking up the members of the set. So to find the interpretation for

owns(John, Misty)

we need to see if the mapping of the objects (John, Misty) is a member of the mapping *owns*. Clearly it is and so the predicate is true in this interpretation. Note that

owns(David, Misty)

is false under the present interpretation since it is not a member of the set.

When expressions with logic connectives are interpreted we follow the same convention as for propositional logic. For instance,

nurse(Sara) ∨ doctor(Sara)

is true if either nurse(Sara) is true or doctor(Sara) is true.

So when we talk of the domain of interpretation, we are really being explicit about the set of objects we are dealing with and the relationships these object take part in.

Example 3.2

Suppose we have the sets

People = {John, David}

Food = {pizza, ice-cream, cake}

and that *likes* is a relation between people and food. What is the maximum number of ordered pairs in this relation?

Solution
Taking the product of the two sets we get

{(John, pizza), (John, ice-cream), (John, cake), (David, pizza),
(David, ice-cream), (David, cake)}

In practice the relation *likes* might be a subset of these ordered pairs since David, for example, might not like cake.

Variables and quantifiers

Suppose *Friday, Misty* and *Teg* are all racehorses and suppose that all of the horses *John* owns are racehorses. How do we represent,

All horses owned by John are racehorses.

Another way of saying this sentence is

If any object is a horse, and that horse is owned by John then it is a racehorse.

We could list all the objects that are horses owned by John and explicitly state that they are racehorses,

(horse(Misty) $\wedge$ owns(John, Misty)) $\rightarrow$ racehorse(Misty)

$\wedge$ (horse(Friday) $\wedge$ owns(John, Friday)) $\rightarrow$ racehorse(Friday)

$\wedge$ (horse(Teg) $\wedge$ owns(John, Teg)) $\rightarrow$ racehorse(Teg)

This is cumbersome and whilst it is true for a particular snapshot in time it is not as general as we would like. For instance, if *John* purchases another horse the above representation has to be expanded. To overcome this limitation, predicate logic has variables and quantifiers. A variable allows us to generalise to a set of objects. In other words, we can make general statements about all objects in a set. If we write

owns(John, x)

where x is a variable, then for the predicate to be true, x will refer to an object that belongs to the set of objects owned by *John*. If we restrict the predicate further with,

horse(x) $\wedge$ owns(John, x)

then x must be a horse and owned by *John*. Note that we could drop 'horse(x)' provided that we make it clear that the domain of x is the set of horses.

Quantifiers allow us to indicate whether we are dealing with all objects in a set or at least one object. When we wish to express that a predicate applies to all the objects we use a universal quantifier denoted by $\forall$. The universal quantifier is read as 'for all' or 'every'. So, returning to our original sentence

All horses owned by John are racehorses.

we write it in predicate notation as

$\forall x.$ (horse(x) $\wedge$ owns(John, x)) $\rightarrow$ racehorse(x).

The other quantifier is known as the 'existential quantifier' denoted by $\exists$. The existential quantifier is interpreted as 'there exists'. For example,

John owns a horse that is a racehorse.

This sentence could be written as

There exists a horse and that horse is owned by John and that horse is a racehorse.

In predicate notation it is written as

$\exists x.\ \text{horse}(x) \wedge \text{owns}(\text{John}, x) \wedge \text{racehorse}(x).$

This is equivalent to writing

$[\text{horse}(\text{Misty}) \wedge \text{owns}(\text{John}, \text{Misty}) \wedge \text{racehorse}(\text{Misty})]$

$\vee\ [\text{horse}(\text{Friday}) \wedge \text{owns}(\text{John}, \text{Friday}) \wedge \text{racehorse}(\text{Friday})]$

$\vee\ [\text{horse}(\text{Teg}) \wedge \text{owns}(\text{John}, \text{Teg}) \wedge \text{racehorse}(\text{Teg})]$

Note that we are not saying that John owns only a single racehorse. We are simply saying that John owns at least one racehorse and so we leave open the possibility of him owning more.

Brackets can be used to make it clear that the quantifier applies to every x in the sentence like so:

$\exists x.\ [\,\text{horse}(x) \wedge \text{owns}(\text{John}, x) \wedge \text{racehorse}(x)].$

There might be some confusion about why we have used implication with the universal quantifier and conjunction with the existential quantifier. Well, in practice, most of the time ($\forall x$) is used with implication and ($\exists x$) with conjunction. For example,

$\forall x.\ [\,\text{horse}(x) \wedge \text{owns}(\text{John}, x) \wedge \text{racehorse}(x)].$

says that **all objects** are racehorses and are owned by John. This statement is too strong and not true. Consider now using the existential quantifier with implication,

$\exists x.\ (\text{horse}(x) \wedge \text{owns}(\text{John}, x)) \rightarrow \text{racehorse}(x).$

This statement is very weak and does not actually say anything at all. If we write out the expression for each object we have,

$(\text{horse}(\text{Misty}) \wedge \text{owns}(\text{John}, \text{Misty})) \rightarrow \text{racehorse}(\text{Misty})$

$\vee\ (\text{horse}(\text{Friday}) \wedge \text{owns}(\text{John}, \text{Friday})) \rightarrow \text{racehorse}(\text{Friday})$

$\vee\ (\text{horse}(\text{Teg}) \wedge \text{owns}(\text{John}, \text{Teg})) \rightarrow \text{racehorse}(\text{Teg})$

The existential expression is true provided at least one of the above (i.e., for Misty or Friday or Teg) sentences is true. From the truth table definition of implication, a sentence is true if both the left-hand side and the right-hand side of the implication is true, or if the left-hand side is false. If therefore we have an object that is not a horse or a horse that is not owned by John, the left-hand side is false and the sentence is true.

Scope of quantifiers

We stated earlier that we can use brackets to make clear the scope of quantification. For example, in

$$\exists x. \, [\, \text{horse}(x) \wedge \text{owns}(\text{John}, x) \wedge \text{racehorse}(x)].$$

x is said to be 'bound' by $\exists x$. The scope of the quantifier $\exists x$ is every x within the square brackets. We could replace x with another variable like y or z provided we obey scoping rules. The concept of scope and variable naming is familiar to programmers. For example, consider the following 'C++' code.

```
#include <iostream.h>
void foo();
void goo();

int x = 2;      //global variable x

void main()
{
   foo();
   goo();
}
void foo()
{
   int x = 5;
   cout << "x = " << x << endl;    //x local to foo()
}
void goo()
{
   int y = 5;
   cout << "x = " << x << endl; //x declared at top of the program
   cout << "y = " << y << endl;
}
```

The output from the program is:

5

2

5

The statement 'int x = 2;' at the top of the program declares the scope of x as the whole program. In foo() a new x is declared and overrides the global x in 'int x = 2;'. The scope of the x in foo() is limited to foo() (no other function can access it). The braces are used in C++ to denote the scope of variables. If we were to rename the variable x in 'int x = 2;' with z then we would also have to rename the x in goo() to avoid an error.

In the expression

$$\forall x. \text{boy}(x) \wedge \text{girl}(y)$$

x is bound but y is free. In the following two expressions both x and y are bound:

$\forall x.\text{boy}(x) \land \exists y.\text{girl}(y)$

$\forall x.\exists y.[\text{boy}(x) \land \text{girl}(y)]$

Suppose we have the expression

$\forall x.\exists y.[p(x, y) \land q(x, y)]$

where p is the property that '$x^2 = y$' and q the property '$x < y$'. Let us restrict the values of x and y to:

$x \in \{2, 4, 6\}$ and $y \in \{4, 9, 16, 25, 36\}$

The set of ordered pairs satisfying p is

$\{(2, 4), (4, 16), (6, 36)\}$

and for q

$\{(2, 4), (2, 9), (2, 16), (2, 25), (2, 36), (4, 9), (4, 16), (4, 25), (4, 36), (6, 9),$
$(6, 16), (6, 25), (6, 36)\}$

We can see that the expression $\forall x.\exists y.[p(x, y) \land q(x, y)]$ is true because it holds for all values of x: x appears as the first argument in an ordered pair of both sets. Suppose now that we change the scope of the expression to

$\forall x.[\exists y.p(x, y) \land q(x, y)]$

We now have y in $q(x, y)$ as a free variable. This means that the y in $q(x, y)$ is free to take on a different value to the y in $p(x, y)$. If $x = 6$ and $y = 36$ then $p(x, y)$ is satisfied but the y in $q(x, y)$ can take on any value from the set $\{4, 9, 16, 25, 36\}$; the expression will not be true in this instance when the y in $q(x, y)$ takes on the value 4 because 6 is not less than 4.

Negation with quantifiers

When using negation, the existential quantifier and universal quantifier have equivalent expression. For instance,

Everyone likes football $\forall x.\ \text{likes}(x, \text{football})$

is the same as saying

There is no one who does not like football $\neg \exists x.\ \neg \text{likes}(x, \text{football})$

There are a set of rules known as De Morgan's rules that express the equivalences between the two quantifiers.

> **De Morgan's rules**
> If P denotes a predicate the rules are:
>
> $$\forall x \neg P \equiv \neg \exists x P$$
>
> $$\neg \forall x P \equiv \exists x \neg P$$
>
> $$\forall x P \equiv \neg \exists x \neg P$$
>
> $$\exists x P \equiv \neg \forall x \neg P$$

Quantifiers can be combined in expressions. For example,

$$\forall x. \exists y \; mother(y, x)$$

says that everyone has a mother. Notice that two variables are required since both arguments need to refer to different objects (i.e., someone cannot be their own mother).

Example 3.3

Express the following sentences in predicate logic.
1. All basketball players are tall.
2. There is a tall basketball player.
3. There is no-one who is both a boy and a girl.
4. Debbie is a pretty girl.
5. No horse owned by John is old.

Solution
1. $\forall x. \; basketball\_player(x) \rightarrow tall(x)$
2. $\exists x. \; basketball\_player(x) \wedge tall(x)$.
3. $\neg \exists x. \; boy(x) \wedge girl(x)$.
4. $pretty(Debbie) \wedge girl(Debbie)$.
5. $\forall x. \; (horse(x) \wedge owns(John, x)) \rightarrow \neg old(x)$.

3.1

? Answers appear in Appendix A.

1 Use predicate logic to represent the following statements:
   (a) John likes fish.
   (b) John likes fish and chips.
   (c) Sara owns a dog or Sara owns a horse.
   (d) All dogs like bones.
   (e) Some dogs like bones.
   (f) All of the dogs that Sue owns are small.
   (g) Everyone loves somebody.
   (h) There is someone who is loved by everyone.

Validating arguments in predicate notation

Validating arguments expressed in predicate notation is really beyond the scope of this book but this section is included to illustrate the basic process. No exercises are included on this topic.

How is the following argument shown to be valid?

Every person has a date of birth $\Big\}$ Assumptions

John is a person

John has a date of birth   Conclusion

The sentence 'Every person has a date of birth' can be written as

$\forall x.\ \text{person}(x) \rightarrow \text{has\_dateOfbirth}(x).$

Now if we write the domain of objects as

$\{x_1, x_2, ..., x_n\}$ where x_1 is an actual object

We can write

$[\text{person}(x_1) \rightarrow \text{has\_dateOfbirth}(x_1)]$

$\land\ [\text{person}(x_2) \rightarrow \text{has\_dateOfbirth}(x_2)]$

$\vdots$

$\land\ [\text{person}(x_n) \rightarrow \text{has\_dateOfbirth}(x_n)]$

The $\land$ elimination rule introduced in Chapter 1 states that the above expression can be written as a list of assumptions.

$[\text{person}(x_1) \rightarrow \text{has\_dateOfbirth}(x_1)]$

$[\text{person}(x_2) \rightarrow \text{has\_dateOfbirth}(x_2)]$

$\vdots$

$[\text{person}(x_n) \rightarrow \text{has\_dateOfbirth}(x_n)]$

Now since John belongs to the domain of objects we can write

$\text{person}(\text{John}) \rightarrow \text{has\_dateOfbirth}(\text{John})$

$\text{person}(x_1) \rightarrow \text{has\_dateOfbirth}(x_1)$

$\text{person}(x_2) \rightarrow \text{has\_dateOfbirth}(x_2)$

etc.

So now we have

1. person(John) → has_dateOfbirth(John)   assumption
2. person(John)   assumption
3. has_dateOfbirth(John)   using 1 and 2 and modus-ponens

We have entered into a reasoned discussion to justify the way in which we have handled the universal quantifier. There are three inference rules in addition to those introduced for propositional logic.

1. Universal elimination
2. Existential elimination
3. Existential introduction

Universal elimination
The universal quantifier can be eliminated from any sentence by replacing the quantified variable with an instance (i.e., object).

For example, for

$$\forall x.likes(x,Bones),$$

we can use a substitution of any object from the domain (of dogs in this case). For example, Sadie is a dog and so we can substitute Sadie (written as $\{x/Sadie\}$) to give

$$likes(Sadie,Bones).$$

We can eliminate the existential quantifier in a similar manner provided the instance used for the substitution is not used elsewhere.

Existential introduction

From an expression such as

$$likes(Sadie,Bones),$$

we can infer

$$\exists x.likes(x,Bones).$$

This last rule must follow from 'Sadie likes bones' since we now know that 'there exists a dog that likes bones'.

We are now in a position to show the validity of arguments written in predicate notation.

Example 3.4

Show that the following statement is valid.

All object-oriented programs have objects. Wacky is an object-oriented program. Therefore, some programs have objects.

Solution
The component sentences are

All object-oriented programs have objects.

Wacky is an object-oriented program.

Some programs have objects.

We need to be able to represent programs that may not be object oriented. So we shall use a predicate

program(x)

to represent that x is a program. So the predicate forms for each sentence are

$\forall x.$ (object-oriented(x) $\land$ program(x)) $\rightarrow$ has_objects(x)

object-oriented(Wacky) $\land$ program(Wacky)

$\exists y.$ program(y) $\land$ has_objects(y)

Notice that the first and third sentences use different variables because they have different quantifiers.

The complete argument is:

$\forall x.[((\text{object-oriented}(x) \land \text{program}(x)) \rightarrow \text{has\_objects}(x)) \land$

object-oriented(Wacky) $\land$ program(Wacky)]

$\models$

[$\exists y.$ program(y) $\land$ has_objects(y)]

The argument can be shown as valid as follows:
1. $\forall x.$ (object-oriented(x) $\land$ program(x)) $\rightarrow$ has_objects(x)   assumption
2. (object-oriented(Wacky) $\land$ program(Wacky))   assumption and
   $\rightarrow$ has_objects(Wacky)   universal elimination

3. object-oriented(Wacky) $\wedge$ program(Wacky)   } assumption
4. has_objects(Wacky)   } using 2 and 3 and modus-ponens
5. program(Wacky)   3 and $\wedge$ elimination
6. program(Wacky) $\wedge$ has_objects(Wacky)   4, 5 and $\wedge$ introduction
7. $\exists y.$ program(y) $\wedge$ has_objects(y)   6 and existential introduction

Summary

Predicate logic can be used to represent the relationships between objects. Predicate logic allows generalised expressions through the use of variables and quantifiers. A constant is a named individual object. A predicate takes the form of

$$predicate\_name(\text{arg}_1, \text{arg}_2, ..., \text{arg}_n)$$

The predicate name starts with a lower-case character. A predicate takes one or more arguments and an argument can be a constant or a variable or a function. The number of arguments is called the arity. A function relates one object to exactly one other object. There are three inference rules in addition to those used for propositional logic.

1. Universal elimination
2. Existential elimination
3. Existential introduction

Application of logic to computing

Logic is used in a large number of computing disciplines. This section will point to a few application areas of logic.

Formal reasoning

Logic can be used for inferencing (i.e., to infer some information not explicitly stated in the text). Formal inferencing is the procedure used to derive or show that a conclusion is valid and the procedure uses the rules of inference introduced in Chapter 1.

Example 3.5

We are told the following:

> If a car has a flat battery then it will not start. If John's car will not start and it is after 8 a.m. then John will miss the train. One morning after 8 a.m. John's car had a flat battery.

Using inference rules of logic show that John missed the train.

Solution
The information can be symbolised as

P – car has flat battery.

Q – car will not start.

R – after 8 a.m.

S – John has missed the train.

Rule 1 $P \rightarrow Q$

Rule 2 $Q \wedge R \rightarrow S$

We are given P and R as TRUE. The task is to prove S. The proof proceeds as

step 1. P	(given as a fact)
step 2. R	(given as a fact)
step 3. Q	From step 1, and rule 1 using modus-ponens
step 4. $Q \wedge R$	From steps 3 and 2, and using And-introduction
step 5. S	From step 4 and rule 2 using modus-ponens.

Expert systems

An expert system is a computer program that has built-in knowledge of a domain expert and can assist with the daily duties of that expert. For example, an expert system might have built-in knowledge about heart disease and can be used to assist a nurse in early diagnosis of a patient and to recommend whether or not a doctor needs to be consulted. An expert system is based on predicate logic and the program will use the rules of inference to prove conclusions although an expert systems program code appears less formal than presented here. The knowledge in an expert system will typically be represented using easy-to-read English-style rules of the form

If condition Then conclusion.

Many expert systems have been built using Prolog.

Prolog

Prolog is a language based on predicate logic. Prolog has traditionally been thought of as a language for implementing artificial intelligence applications but more recently it has been used as a general programming language. Prolog is not like a conventional programming language in which you specify the format of information and how the solution should be arrived at; it is usual when programming to specify the procedure or method for solving the task at hand. Prolog, though, is a 'declarative' language, which means that a program is written as a series of statements and rules. Prolog has an inferencing facility that can be fed these statements to perform the desired computation. In other words, we build a program from specifying information and what we require from the program but not how to perform the task.

The syntax of Prolog is based on predicate logic. A relationship such as 'John loves Mary' is written as

love(john, mary).

The predicate (i.e., relation) and objects of the relationship must begin with a lower-case letter. The above relationship is treated as a fact and other examples of facts are:

metal(copper).   copper is a metal

play(john, mary, tennis).   john and mary play tennis

A variable begins with an upper-case character. When a variable refers to a constant (that is, an actual instance, e.g., john), the variable is said to be instantiated. A variable can be instantiated when expressions match. For example, suppose the database (the collection of facts and rules) holds *love(john, mary)*. The following questions can be asked:

loves(X, mary).   Who loves mary?

answer X = john.   X is instantiated to john

love(john, X).   Who is it that john loves?

answer X = mary.   X is instantiated to mary

love(X, Y).   Who loves who?

answer X = john, Y = mary.

Rules in Prolog are expressed using a backward notation in the form 'conclusion if condition' as opposed to 'if condition then conclusion'. For example,

uncle(X, Y) :- father(Z, Y), brother(Z, X).

The term ':-' stands for IF and the term ',' stands for AND. So the above rule states that

X is Y's uncle IF Z is Y's father AND Z is the brother of X.

An example instantiation of this rule is shown in Figure 3.1.

A variable is local to a clause (i.e., a fact or rule); a variable with the same name appearing in two different rules will be treated by Prolog as having different names.

Prolog works by unification. When Prolog attempts to prove a goal it will search for the first clause that can be matched. For a match, two clauses must

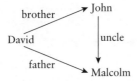

uncle(john, malcolm):- father(david, malcolm), brother(david, john).

Figure 3.1 Prolog rule that is satisfied by the semantic representation shown in the above diagram

- have the same relation
- have the same number of arguments
- match on each argument.

Arguments match according to

1. Constant match. Two constants match if they are identical strings.
2. Constant with a variable. If a variable is not instantiated then the variable will match any constant and will be instantiated to that constant. An instantiated variable will match a constant according to 1.
3. Two variables. Two free variables (i.e., not instantiated) always match and if at a later stage one variable becomes instantiated to a constant then the other variable will also be instantiated to that constant.

Example matches are shown in Table 3.1

Table 3.1

Expression 1	Expression 2	Match
love(john, mary)	love(john, mary)	yes
love(john, X)	love(john, mary)	X=mary
love(john, mary)	like(john, mary)	no
love(X, Y)	love(john, mary)	X=john Y=mary
love(john, mary)	love(X, X)	no
love(X, mary) and X=john	love(Y, mary)	Y=X=john
hit(john, chris)	hit(john, chris, stick)	no

Example 3.6

Given the Prolog program listed below explain how Prolog answers

?-uncle(john, X). The ?- is Prolog's prompt

Program listing:

1. father(david, malcolm).
2. uncle(graham, malcolm).
3. brother(david, john).
4. uncle(X, Y) :- father(Z, Y), brother(Z, X).

Line numbers are shown for convenience.

Solution
Prolog searches for a clause with the predicate uncle and two arguments. The first occurrence is found at line 2 but the match fails because the first argument graham does not match john. The second clause containing uncle is found at line 4 but for Prolog to succeed in proving its goal (the goal is to show that John is someone's uncle) the right-hand side of the clause must be satisfied: there needs to be a match for father(Z, Y) and brother(Z, X). The X in the query is treated as being different to the X in the rule and so we have:

Query: uncle(john, X1)

To be matched against: uncle(X2, Y) which is the head of the rule at line 4.

There is a match with X2 = john and Y = X1 (or X1 = Y). The task is now to prove father(Z, X1) and brother(Z, john). The father(Z, X1) matches line 1 with Z = david and X1 = malcolm. The task now is to prove brother(david, john) which is satisfied by line 3. Prolog responds with X=malcolm.

Natural language processing

There are many applications that would benefit from the ability to process and understand information expressed in English. For one thing, such a facility can make a system easier to use. A front-end query system to a database that takes requests in everyday English is a typical application for natural language processing. It is a difficult task to program even a limited natural language processing facility. Consider the following passage.

> John entered the restaurant. He ordered lobster and salad. He finished his meal with a cup of coffee, paid the bill and left the waiter a tip.

With little effort we could answer questions such as:

Who ordered lobster?

Who cooked the lobster?

Why did John leave the waiter a tip?

Imagine building a computer system to answer these questions. For the first question we might try for a simple solution using pattern matching,

> Who ordered lobster

> He ordered lobster

Of course, 'He' is not the answer we are looking for. Also the question might have been expressed as

> The lobster was ordered by Whom?

So simple pattern matching is not the answer.

The second question asks about cooking but the text makes no mention of cooking. To answer this question and the third question requires general knowledge of the domain (in this case a restaurant domain) and this is knowledge we gain from experience.

A natural language processing system has to represent general domain knowledge. The system also has to extract information from a text and represent it in such a way that it can process queries. Logic is often used for the formal representation of knowledge in natural language processing systems.

Formal specification and verification of programs

It is typical for the requirements of a computer system to be expressed in English. A formal specification will represent the information contained in the requirements document in a way that clarifies what is needed. The process of formally specifying a system reduces ambiguity by bringing to light questions that need to be asked of the customer.

A formal specification can be used for formal reasoning to explore a system's behaviour before any code is implemented. This reasoning can highlight where the design model needs changing. Identifying a change before implementation in code can save costly rework. Formal reasoning is also used to validate a formal model against the requirements. For example, programmers use program functions that are contained in a library. A library function can be specified in a contractual sense, such that the function will guarantee to return data that satisfies a set of postconditions provided that the programmer (library user) ensures that input data satisfies a set of preconditions. Formal methods can be used to verify that a function will satisfy its postconditions if the preconditions are met.

All programming languages have what are known as conditional expressions which means that in order for certain code to execute then a condition must be satisfied. The following piece of code is from the 'C' language:

```
if(x ! = y)
    x = y;
```

The != means not equal to. Let us take the variables x and y to be integers. The piece of code simply states that if x and y are not equal then x should be set to the same value as y – the expression is

If x is not the same value as y Then set x to the same value as y

The value for x before the conditional statement could be

equal to y or

less than y or

greater than y

If we are given the task of testing the above piece of code then we might set up a file of test data and try to ensure that the code does what is intended under all possible situations. In practice we cannot look at every situation since there are an infinite number of values that can be assigned to x and y. We can, though, test the logic for the three possibilities: equal to, less than, greater than. The table below gives a possible test scenario with results:

Start value of x	Value of y	Final value of x
−1	2	2
3	2	2
2	2	2

The code can be expressed in logic and is of the form:

$$P \rightarrow Q$$

with P symbolising $x \mathrel{!}= y$ and Q $x = y$. If instead we symbolise P as $x = y$ we can represent the code as:

$$\neg P \rightarrow P$$

If we produce the truth table for $\neg P \rightarrow P$ we find that $\neg P \rightarrow P$ is equivalent to P. This tells us that at the end of this block of code we have $x = y$ which is what was intended. It also shows that we might as well replace the block of code with simply $x = y$. Of course this is a trivial example but in more complicated blocks of code there is a real likelihood of redundant code. On every occasion that a program needs to check a statement, time is taken up and for certain applications time is critical. There are automated tools for highlighting blocks of code that take a long time to execute. It might be possible to inspect any blocks of code that are highlighted and recode them in a more efficient manner. We shall consider another simple example.

What is the following code doing?

```
1. if(x ! = y){
2.     if(x < y)
3.         x = y;
4. }
```

Let us inspect the output using our test table:

Start value of x	Value of y	End value of x
-1	2	2
3	2	3
2	2	2

Suppose that someone suggests that this code is equivalent to

```
if(x < y)
    x = y;
```

Again we shall inspect our test table for this code:

Start value of x	Value of y	End value of x
-1	2	2
3	2	3
2	2	2

We could use logic to see if these blocks of code are equivalent. Let

P symbolise $x = y$

Q symbolise $x < y$

The original code is then

$$\neg P \rightarrow (Q \rightarrow P)$$

The new code is

$$Q \rightarrow P$$

We shall test for equivalence using the truth table

P	Q	$\neg P$	$Q \to P$	$\neg P \to (Q \to P)$
T	T	F	T	T
F	T	T	F	F
T	F	F	T	T
F	F	T	T	T

We see that the fifth and fourth columns are the same and so the versions of code are equivalent.

Logic circuit design

Computer hardware consists of small logic units called gates, that take inputs and give outputs that are 0s and 1s (i.e., binary). These gates implement what are known as Boolean functions. For example, there are gates for AND, OR, XOR, etc. The definitions of these functions are familiar from our earlier introduction except that different symbols are sometimes used. Some definitions are given below.

x	y	$x \vee y$ OR	xy AND	$x \otimes y$ XOR
1	1	1	1	0
1	0	1	0	1
0	1	1	0	1
0	0	0	0	0

Logic gates are combined to implement certain fundamental operations. As an example, we shall take a look at adding integer values. Assuming a representation of eight bits, the number 11 is binary 00001011, and the number 9 is binary 00001001. The addition in binary is given by:

$$
\begin{array}{r}
00001011 \\
00001001 \\
\hline
00010100
\end{array}
$$

Addition in binary is similar to decimal addition. The digits are added in each column working from right to left. If the sum is greater than 1, 0 is written and a 1 is carried to the next column. Only two digits are handled at a time and the combinations are

$$\begin{pmatrix} 1 & 1 & 0 & 0 \\ 1 & 0 & 1 & 0 \\ \overline{0} & \overline{1} & \overline{1} & \overline{0} \end{pmatrix}$$

where the bottom row is the sum of the two digits above. The result of the bottom row can be seen as the XOR of the two digits being summed. A carry of 1 will occur when the two digits to be summed are both 1. The AND of two bits is 1. So the sum to be written can be executed with an XOR gate and the carry with an AND gate as shown in Figure 3.2. This circuit is known as a half-adder and by complementing this circuit with a few more logic gates, full binary addition is possible.

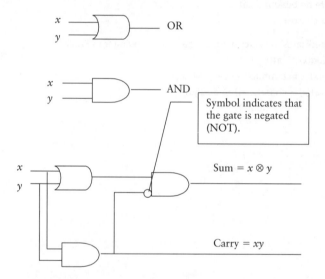

Figure 3.2   Half-adder circuit. Notice that XOR has been constructed out of two gates (i.e., OR gate combined with NOT AND (NAND)).

EXERCISES

Answers appear in Appendix B.

1 For the sets:
man = {David, John}
woman = {Brenda, Sheila, Janet}
husband-of = {(David, Brenda), (John, Janet)}
lives-with = {(David, Brenda), (John, Janet), (David, Sheila)}

Which of the following statements is true?

(a) man(David)

(b) man(David) ∨ woman(David)

(c) man(David) ∧ ¬woman(David)

(d) lives-with(David,Sheila) → ¬woman(David)

(e) lives-with(David,Sheila) → husband – of(David,Sheila)

2 Given the following predicates

dog(x) – x is a dog, cat(x) – x is a cat, eat(x, meat) – x eats meat

beautiful(x) – x is beautiful, chase(x, y) – x chases y

Translate the following into symbols.

(a) Some dogs eat meat

(b) All dogs eat meat

(c) Nothing is both a cat and a dog

(d) There are beautiful dogs

(e) There are no beautiful cats

(f) All dogs chase a cat

3 Using the predicates in Exercise 2 translate the following into English.

(a) $\forall x.\neg[\text{dog}(x) \land \text{cat}(x)]$

(b) $\forall x.[\text{dog}(x) \land \text{beautiful}(x) \rightarrow \text{eat}(x,\text{Meat})]$

(c) $\forall x \forall y.[(\text{cat}(x) \land \text{chase}(y, x)) \rightarrow \text{dog}(y)]$

(d) $\forall x.[\text{eat}(x, \text{meat}) \rightarrow \text{dog}(x)]$

4

Relations and functions

Introduction

Relations and functions are fundamental concepts for the modelling of information in computer systems. We have already met these terms in Chapter 3 but in this chapter we take a more formal look at relations and functions. The material in this chapter is useful for understanding the technological description of many computing topics like logic, image processing, fuzzy systems, object-oriented modelling, databases, etc. The main purpose of this chapter is to introduce some key terms and the concepts that these terms are referring to.

Relations

We have already met relations in Chapter 3 but we called them predicates. For example, the relation *love* between two objects in 'John loves Mary' could be represented using predicate notation as

love(John, Mary).

The relationship *love* takes two arguments and is therefore a binary relationship. Because we are so familiar with family relationships they are useful in exploring some of the more formal concepts about relations that will be introduced later. Consider the family tree in Figure 4.1. Sometimes we express a relation in terms of other relations. For example, we can see that David is the uncle of Bill. We could deduce this uncle relationship from being told that Brian is the father of Bill and David is the brother of Brian. So we could express the relationship *uncle* in terms of the relations *father* and *brother*. If we examine the children of David we see that they are all female. If we are concerned only with the set of David's children then the *sister of* relation is 'symmetric' which means that if we are given 'Mary is the sister of Jane' we can write 'Jane is the sister of Mary' and we can do this for each object in the set (i.e., each of David's children). Note that the *sister of* relation is not symmetric for the set of Brian's children because although 'Sara is the sister of Bill' it is incorrect to say 'Bill is the sister of Mary'. Consider next the relation *same sex as*. If we consider the set of David's children and list the objects which are 'the same sex as Mary' then

Mary would appear in that list. We can repeat this for 'the same sex as Jane' and 'the same sex as Debbie'. If for some relation, every member of a set is related to itself then the relation is said to be 'reflexive'. So the relation *is sister of* is reflexive for the set of David's children. The final relation that we shall consider in Figure 4.1 is *descendant of*. David, Mary, Jane and Debbie are descendants of David, and David, Brian, Mary, Jane, Debbie, Bill and Sara are descendants of John. We know that if '*x* is a descendant of *y* and *y* is a descendant of *z* then *x* is a descendant of *z*'. Such a relation is known as a 'transitive' relation.

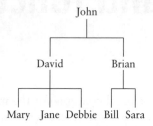

Figure 4.1   A family tree

So far we have considered only family relations but we can define an endless number of relations between objects that are not people. For example, we might consider the relationship *works for* that applies to a set of companies and a set of employees. The relation *less than* can be defined over the set of integers. Binary relations occur very frequently but a relation can take any number of arguments. For example, if we wish to describe the departure of a train from a station we might want to define *departure* as a ternary (three arguments) relationship that gives the final destination, the platform where the train leaves from, and the time of departure.

Defining relations

Relations can be defined in a number of ways. If natural language (everyday English) is to be used then 'infix' notation is used. For a binary relation, infix notation is of the form

$a R b$

where *a* and *b* are objects and *R* is a relation. An example is

John loves Mary.

Let us look at another example of a binary relation – the *works for* relation. Suppose we have the following facts:

Mary works for Cigol

David works for Cigol

Bill works for Cigol

Sara works for Golorp

John works for Golorp

All of the above people are employees and so we shall consider two sets: the set E of employees and the set C of companies.

$E = \{$Mary, David, Bill, Sara, John$\}$

$C = \{$Cigol, Golorp$\}$

Next we shall write down the set of products $E \times C$

$E \times C = \{$(Mary, Cigol), (Mary, Golorp), (David, Cigol), (David, Golorp), (Bill, Cigol), (Bill, Golorp), (Sara, Cigol), (Sara, Golorp), (John, Cigol), (John, Golorp)$\}$

If we were to write down the power set of $E \times C$, which is the set of all subsets of $E \times C$, we would find that a member of this power set is

$\{$(Mary, Cigol), (David, Cigol), (Bill, Cigol) (Sara, Golorp), (John, Golorp)$\}$

Each ordered pair in the above set gives the objects that fit the relation *works for*. Remember that the order of arguments matters and that is why we use ordered pairs; we could not write

Cigol works for Mary.

We can see from the above example that a relation between a set A and a set B is a subset of

$A \times B$

Also, we see that the relation is a member of the power set of $A \times B$.

So, a binary relation, R, can be written as a set of ordered pairs. This leads to another way of expressing

$a \, R \, b$

as

$(a, b) \in R$

which states that the ordered pair (a, b) belongs to the relation R.

Example 4.1

Given that

$$S = \{3, 2, 5\}$$

give the set of ordered pairs that satisfy the relation

$$x < y$$

where $<$ is 'less than'.

Solution
The set of ordered pairs is

$$S \times S = \{(3,3), (3,2), (3,5), (2,3), (2,2), (2,5), (5,3), (5,2), (5,5)\}$$

Each ordered pair can be examined to see if it conforms to

$x < y$
$3 < 3$	False
$3 < 2$	False
$3 < 5$	True
$2 < 3$	True
$2 < 2$	False
$2 < 5$	True
$5 < 3$	False
$5 < 2$	False
$5 < 5$	False

and so the relation is the set of ordered pairs

$$\{(3,5),(2,3),(2,5)\}$$

Example 4.2

Given that

$$S = \{3, 2, 5\}$$

give the set of ordered pairs that satisfy the relation

$$x \leq y$$

where $\leq$ is 'less than or equal to'.

Solution
The relation has a set of ordered pairs which is a subset of the product $S \times S$ given in Example 4.1; each ordered pair, (x, y), must have x less than or equal to y. So the set is:

$\{(3,5),(2,3),(2,5), (2,2), (3,3), (5,5)\}$

4.1

Answers appear in Appendix A.

1 Given that

$S = \{1, 2, 3\}$

(a) give the set of ordered pairs that satisfy the relation

$(x + y) = 5$

(b) give the set of ordered pairs that satisfy the relation

$(x + y) > 2$

2 A binary relation R is defined on the set S. Which of the following statements must be false?

$S = \{John, Sara, Debbie\}$

(a) (John,John) $\in R$
(b) (John,Debbie) $\in R$
(c) (Debbie,Brian) $\in R$

Properties of Relations

There are a number of properties that are of interest to us when dealing with binary relations of a single set. Three of these properties were introduced at the start of this chapter:

1. Reflexive
2. Symmetric
3. Transitive

In this section we shall explain more fully each of these properties.

Reflexive

> If a relation R on a set S is reflexive, then each member x of the set S appears as an ordered pair (x, x) in $S \times S$.

The above definition can be stated more formally as

$x \in S \rightarrow (x,x) \in R$

Example 4.3

Given that

$$S = \{3, 2, 5\}$$

is the relation $x \leq y$ reflexive on the set S?

Solution
For the relation to be reflexive all ordered pairs of the form (x, x) must appear in $S \times S$: so the following pairs must appear

$$(3,3),(2,2),(5,5)$$

We know from Example 4.2 that these pairs do appear and therefore the relation is reflexive.

Example 4.4

Given the set

{John, Mary, Sara}

is the relation *same sex as* reflexive?

Solution
The relation *same sex as* has the set of ordered pairs

{(John, John), (Mary, Mary), (Mary, Sara), (Sara, Sara), (Sara, Mary)}

The following pairs

(John, John), (Mary, Mary), (Sara, Sara)

are all present in the set and so the relation is reflexive.

Symmetric

> If a relation is symmetric, then wherever the ordered pair (a, b) appears the pair (b, a) should also appear.

The more formal definition is

$$[x, y \in S \wedge (x, y) \in R] \rightarrow (y, x) \in R$$

Note that it is incorrect to express the symmetric property as

$$[x, y \in S \rightarrow [(x, y) \in R \wedge (y, x) \in R]$$

since this states that every ordered pair of the set S should appear in R.

Example 4.5

Given that

$$S = \{3, 2, 5\}$$

is the relation $x \leq y$ symmetric on the set S?

Solution
The set of ordered pairs that satisfy the relation is

$$\{(3,5),(2,3),(2,5), (2,2), (3,3), (5,5)\}$$

The first pair is (3,5) and for the relation to be symmetric the pair (5,3) should appear in the set. The pair does not appear and therefore the relation is not symmetric.

Example 4.6

Which of the following relations is symmetric on the set $\{3, 5, 6, 7, 8\}$?

1. $\{(3, 6), (6, 7), (8, 7), (7, 6), (7, 8)\}$
2. $\{(3, 7), (3, 8), (8, 3), (7, 3)\}$

Solution
1. This relation is not symmetric since for the first pair (3, 6) we do not find (6, 3) in the set.
2. Symmetric – since for (3, 7), (7, 3) is a member and for (3, 8), (8, 3) is a member and same must be true for the pairs (8, 3) and (7, 3).

Transitive

> If an object a is related to b and b is related to c means that a is related to c then the relation is said to be transitive.

More formally we have

$$[x, y, z \in S \wedge (x, y) \in R \wedge (y, z) \in R] \rightarrow (x, z) \in R$$

Example 4.7

Is the following relation transitive?

$$\{(0,0),(0,2),(0,4),(2,0),(2,2),(2,4),(4,0),(4,2),(4,4),(5,5)\}$$

Solution
If we take the first pair (0, 0) for (*x, y*) we need to check for any pairs of the form
(*y, z*) i.e., (0, *z*) and check that (*x, z*) i.e., (0, *z*) appear:

$$(0,0) \land (0,0) \rightarrow (0,0)$$

$$(0,0) \land (0,2) \rightarrow (0,2)$$

$$(0,0) \land (0,4) \rightarrow (0,4)$$

The definition of the transitive property tells us that for each combination on the left-hand side of → we should find the pair on the right-hand side. Since each pair on the right-hand side of this expression also appears on the left-hand side it must be a member of the set. Consider the pair (0, 2):

$$(0,2) \land (2,0) \rightarrow (0,0)$$

$$(0,2) \land (2,2) \rightarrow (0,2)$$

$$(0,2) \land (2,4) \rightarrow (0,4)$$

All these combinations satisfy the property. If we were to check all other possible combinations we will see that the relation is transitive.

Example 4.8

The following pairs are members of the descendant relation from the set of people in Figure 4.1.

{(Mary, David), (Jane, David), (Debbie, David), (Mary, John), (Jane, John), (Debbie, John), (Bill, Brian), (Sara, Brian), (Bill, John), (Sara, John), (David, John), (Brian, John)}

We already know that this relation is transitive. If for illustration we check the first pair (Mary, David) we should find that whenever we find a pattern

(David, *z*)

we should find

(Mary, *z*)

The only occurrence where David appears as the first argument in a pair is (David, John) and so we should see that (Mary, John) appears as a member of the relation.

Example 4.9

Is the following relation transitive?

{(1,2), (2, 4), (1, 4), (3, 6), (4, 3), (2, 3), (1, 3), (6, 8)}

Solution

A systematic way of checking if a relation is transitive is to create another copy of the relation and align them one underneath each other:

$$\{(1, 2), (2, 4), (1, 4), (3, 6), (4, 3), (2, 3), (1, 3), (6, 8)\}$$
$$\{(1, 2), (2, 4), (1, 4), (3, 6), (4, 3), (2, 3), (1, 3), (6, 8)\}$$

Now we take the first pair (1, 2) in the first copy and look at where the second argument in this pair appears as a first argument in any pair in the second copy. We get

(1, 2)   pair being inspected from first copy

(2, 4), (2, 3)   pairs from second copy whose first argument is 2

Now we form pairs using the first argument of the top row with the second arguments of each pair in the second row to give

(1, 4)(1, 3)

Both of these pairs need to be members of the relation. Both pairs are and so we check the next pair:

(2, 4)   pair being inspected from first copy

(4, 3)   pairs from second copy whose first argument is 4

So (2, 3) should be a member. It is and so we check the third:

(1, 4)   pair being inspected from first copy

(4, 3)   pairs from second copy whose first argument is 4

So (1, 3) should be a member and it is. Checking the fourth

(3, 6)   pair being inspected from first copy

(6, 8)   pairs from second copy whose first argument is 6

(3, 8) is not a member and so the relation is not transitive.

Example 4.10

There is a binary relation between an integer m and an integer n in which we say 'm is congruent to n modulo p', written as $m \equiv n(\mathrm{mod}\ p)$ provided that $m - n$ is a multiple of p where p is taken to be a fixed integer that is greater than 1. Another way of seeing whether a pair of numbers satisfy this relation is to check that both numbers have the same remainder when divided by p. For example, the integer 8 is congruent to 4 modulo 2 since $8 - 4$ $(=4)$ is a multiple of 2. The integer 15 is congruent to 6 modulo 3 since $15 - 6 = 9$ and 9 is a multiple of 3.

Given the set

$$S = \{0, 2, 4, 6\}$$

find the ordered pairs that satisfy the relation

$$a \equiv b(\bmod 2)$$

Is the relation symmetric? Is the relation reflexive? Is the relation transitive?

Solution

First we shall write down the set of ordered pairs

$S \times S = \{(0,0),(0,2),(0,4),(0,6),(2,0),(2,2),(2,4),(2,6),(4,0),(4,2),(4,4),(4,6),$
$(6,0),(6,2),(6,4),(6,6)\}$

So, examining each pair we have

$0 - 0 = 0$

$0 - 2 = -2$

$0 - 4 = -4$

$0 - 6 = -6$

$2 - 0 = 2$

$2 - 2 = 0$

$2 - 4 = -2$

$2 - 6 = -4$

$4 - 0 = 4$

$4 - 2 = 2$

$4 - 4 = 0$

$4 - 6 = -2$

$6 - 0 = 6$

$6 - 2 = 4$

$6 - 4 = 2$

$6 - 6 = 0$

So the pairs whose difference is a multiple of 2 are all of the pairs in

$S \times S$

If the relation is symmetric we should see that if the pair (x, y) belong to R then so does (y, x). For example $(0, 2)$ is a member and therefore $(2, 0)$ should be a member. In fact if we check each pair we see that the property holds and therefore the relation is symmetric.

If the relation is reflexive on S then we should see that the pairs $(0, 0)$, $(2, 2)$, $(4, 4)$ and $(5, 5)$ are members of the relation. Indeed they are and so the relation is reflexive.

If the relationship is transitive we should find that for each pair (a, b) if there is a pair (b, c) then there must be a pair (a, c). For example, for the pair $(2, 4)$ there is a pair $(4, 0)$, $(4, 2)$, $(4, 4)$ and $(4, 6)$ and there must be pairs $(2, 0)$, $(2, 2)$, $(2, 4)$ and $(2, 6)$ for the relation to be transitive. If we check each pair we shall see that the relation is transitive.

> If a relation is reflexive, symmetric and transitive, then it is an 'equivalence' relation. The relation $m \equiv n(\mod p)$ on the set of integers is an equivalence relation.

One other type of property defines an **antisymmetric** relation.

> If for two different objects a and b we have aRb but cannot have bRa then the relation is 'antisymmetric'. Another way of looking at this property is to say that if we find the pairs (a, b) and (b, a) as members of the relation then a must be equal to b for the relation to be antisymmetric.

More formally

$$[x, y \in S \wedge (x, y) \in R \wedge (y, x) \in R] \rightarrow x = y$$

Example 4.11

Which of the following relations is antisymmetric?

1. $\{(1, 1), (2, 3), (2, 2)\}$
2. $\{(1, 1), (2, 3), (2, 2), (3, 2)\}$

Solution
1. Antisymmetric.

2. Not antisymmetric since we have $(2, 3)$ and $(3, 2)$ and 2 does not equal 3.

> A binary relation on a set S that is reflexive, antisymmetric and transitive is called a 'partial ordering' on S.

Example 4.12

Given that

$$S = \{3, 2, 5\}$$

is the relation $x \leq y$ antisymmetric on the set S?

Solution
The ordered pairs satisfying the relation are:

$$\{(3,5),(2,3),(2,5),\ (2,2),\ (3,3),\ (5,5)\}$$

Therefore the relation is antisymmetric.

Properties are useful for identifying ways in which computing storage space can be saved. For example, if we know that each ordered pair in a set is symmetric then for each pair (x, y) we do not need to store (y, x). Knowing that objects take part in a transitive relation also allows us to save storage and to infer properties. Inheritance is one of the fundamental relationships used in consticting what are known as object-oriented models. Inheritance is a transitive relationship and is a useful concept in structuring a model of some computer systems. If we define attributes and functions for an object then these attributes and functions need only be written once and they can be inherited by a child object. In the 1960s some psychologists suggested that humans store information in a hierarchical fashion. For example, a canary can be considered to inherit properties from 'bird' which in turn inherits properties from 'animal'. So if we know that:

> Animal has properties: breathes, eats, has skin
>
> Bird has properties: has wings, can fly, has feathers
>
> Canary: can sing, is yellow

then we can infer that a bird can breathe, eats, and has skin because it is a type of animal (i.e., it inherits these properties). Also we can infer that a canary has wings, can fly, has feathers, breathes, eats and has skin because a canary is a type of bird and therefore is a type of animal. We save storage because we do not have to list the animal properties explicitly for bird and we do not have to list the animal and bird properties explicitly for canary. Psychologists supported their theory for the way in which we might store information by performing timing experiments with human subjects. For example, it took longer for someone to answer 'Does a canary have skin?' than it did for 'Can a canary sing?' The explanation for the difference in time to respond was that 'has skin' is stored further away from the concept of animal compared to 'can sing' which is stored with the concept of canary: in other words the answer to 'Does a canary have skin?' has to be inferred from bird which in turn needs to be inferred from animal and hence requires more time.

Equivalence is an important concept when dealing with 'types' in computing. An object that belongs to the set of integers is a type of integer, an object that belongs to the set of cars is a type of car. One of the great attractions of object-oriented programming is that we are free to create our own types. The facility for creating types means that we can construct computer models that are more representative of the real-world process that we are programming. We can use a basic example to indicate how equivalence relations are a useful concept for dealing with types. Consider a restaurant menu that has ice-cream on the dessert menu and the option of a coffee to follow:

{strawberry, vanilla, toffee, Coffee}

So we have three types of ice-cream and one type of drink. A customer can order a double portion of any of the items, so you can can have a double-size vanilla ice-cream or you can mix the ice-cream. You can have a double-size coffee as a drink. So the relation *double-portion* can be represented by the ordered pairs:

{(strawberry, strawberry), (strawberry, vanilla), (strawberry, toffee),

(vanilla, strawberry), (vanilla, vanilla), (vanilla, toffee),

(toffee, strawberry), (toffee, vanilla), (toffee, toffee),

(Coffee, Coffee)}

It might seem a little artificial to include instances like (strawberry, vanilla) and (vanilla, strawberry) but we are allowing for the possibility that some customers are particular about the order of presentation. The relation is an equivalence relation and could be written as

({strawberry, vanilla, toffee} $\times$ {strawberry, vanilla, toffee})

$\cup$

({coffee} $\times$ {coffee})

The original set can also be written as

{strawberry, vanilla, toffee}$\cup${coffee}

So the original set can be partitioned {{strawberry, vanilla, toffee},{coffee}} and the partition is associated with the relation. The partition in this example splits the set members into their two types (ice-cream and drink).

The use of equivalence classes also has an application within image processing for labelling pixels in connected regions.

The concept of ordered relations in computing is useful because there are many instances where the ordering of items matters. For example, the order of words in a dictionary.

4.2

Answers appear in Appendix A.

1 For each of the following relations, say whether the relation is:

reflexive

symmetric

transitive

(a) {(1, 3), (2, 5), (5, 2), (3, 1)} on the set {1, 2, 3, 5}

(b) {(1, 2), (2, 4), (1, 4), (2, 5), (1, 5)} on the set {1, 2, 4, 5}

(c) {(Red, Orange), (Orange, Yellow), (Red, Yellow), (Yellow, Green), (Orange, Green), (Red, Green)} on the set {Red, Orange, Yellow, Green}

(d) {(1, 2), (1, 1), (2, 1), (2, 2)} on the set {1, 2}

(e) {(Dave, John), (Dave, Bruce), (John, Dave), (John, Bruce), (Bruce, Dave), (Bruce, John), (John, John), (Dave, Dave), (Bruce, Bruce)} on the set {Dave, John, Bruce}

Functions

From our study of maths at school we are familiar with the idea of plotting a function. The function $y = x^2$ is a curve when plotted as shown in Figure 4.2. The curves in Figure 4.2 have been plotted over a range of values of x. If we take a value for x we can read off the curve to find the value of y. It is more general to write this function in the form

$$f(x) = x^2$$

We can evaluate (i.e., calculate the output for) this function for several values of x:

$$f(-4) = 16$$

$$f(-1) = 1$$

$$f(1) = 1$$

$$f(3) = 9$$

We have evaluated the function for only a few integer values but of course we could input any real number like $\{-1.29, 45.6, ...\}$ and because the input can be any real number there are an infinite number of possible inputs.

A function can also be viewed as a system that takes input and produces some output. We could write down a set of ordered pairs of the form (input, output):

$$\{(-4, 16), (-1, 1), (1, 1), (3, 9),...\}$$

Because there are an infinite number of possibilities we could better describe the associated pairs of input/output using set notation

$$\{(x, f(x)) \mid f(x) = x^2\}$$

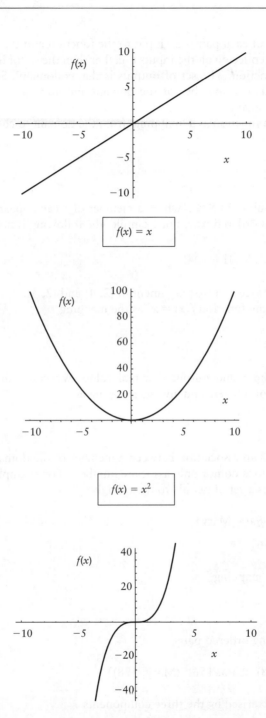

Figure 4.2   Some sample function plots.

The first argument of each pair is an input to the function and the second argument is the output. If we collected all the inputs together then the set of inputs is called the 'domain' of the function. The set of outputs is the 'codomain'. So any object that serves as input will be a member of the domain and any output object will be a member of the codomain.

We also talk of a function as a 'mapping' from the domain to codomain and write it as

$$f : S \to T$$

This mapping is a subset of $S \times T$ where a member of S can appear only once as the first argument of an ordered pair. For example, the following is not a function

$$\{(2, 4), (3, 8), (2, 5)\}$$

because 2 appears twice as a first argument in $(2, 4)$ and $(2, 5)$.

We could write the function $f(x) = x^2$ as the mapping

$$f : R \to R$$

to state that the input and output is a real value. We could instead restrict the function to the set of integers and give its mapping as

$$f : Z \to Z$$

The function acts as an association between a member of the domain and a member of the range. Functions do not only associate numbers. For example, we might have a function that maps a set of people to their height:

$$L = \{\text{George, Sara, Mary}\}$$

$$M = \{178, 156\}$$

Our function is the mapping

$$f : L \to M$$

and has the following ordered pairs

$$\{(\text{George, } 178), (\text{Sara, } 156), (\text{Mary, } 178)\}$$

A function is characterised by the three components

1. Domain
2. Codomain
3. Description of how to compute the function.

Example 4.13

Which of the following is a function?

1. $f: S \to T$ with $S = \{5, 6, 7\}$ and $T = \{9, 2, 1\}$ and $f = \{(5, 9), (6, 1), (7, 2)\}$

2. $f: S \to T$ with $S = \{5, 6, 7\}$ and $T = \{9, 2, 1\}$ and $f = \{(5, 9), (6, 1), (6, 2)\}$

3. $f: S \to T$ with $S = \{5, 6, 7\}$ and $T = \{9, 2, 1\}$ and $f = \{(5, 7), (6, 1), (7, 2)\}$

4. $g: S \to S$ with $S = \{5, 6, 7\}$ $g = \{(5, 6), (7, 5), (6, 6)\}$

5. $g: Z \to Z$ and $g(x) = x - 7$

6. $g: Z \to N$ and $g(x) = x - 7$

Solutions

1. Function.

2. Not a function because 6 appears as a first argument twice.

3. Not a function because 7 in the pair (5, 7) is not a member of the codomain.

4. Function.

5. Function.

6. Not a function because $g(5) = -2$ and -2 is not a member of the domain of non-negative integers. Note that any counter example could be used to show that this example is not a function.

We will often see that a function does not always output every member of the codomain. For example,

$$f: N \to N \qquad f(x) = x + 2$$

has as domain and codomain the set

$$\{0, 1, 2, 3, 4, 5, 6, \ldots\}$$

The function includes the pairs

$$\{(1, 3), (2, 4), (3, 5), \ldots\}$$

Notice that the numbers 1 and 2 never appear as outputs even though they are members of the codomain. The members of the codomain that can appear as outputs are members of the 'range'; the range is a subset of the codomain. So any member of the domain can serve as input but not every member of the codomain need be a valid output (only those members of the range). We can sketch the association of these sets as shown in Figure 4.3

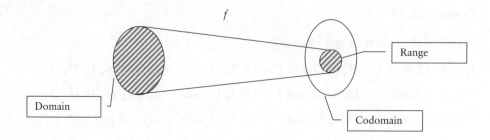

$$f(x) = x + 2$$

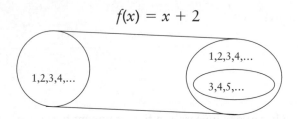

Figure 4.3   Diagram illustrating the domain, codomain and range

One-one functions and onto functions

Two functions f and g have the following definitions

$f : Z \rightarrow Z \quad f(x) = x^2$

$g : N \rightarrow N \quad g(x) = x^2$

The function f can give the same output for different inputs. For example $f(-1) = 1$ and $f(1) = 1$. The function g will never produce the same output for different inputs.

> If a distinct input always gives a distinct output then the function is one–one (one to one) or 'injective'. In other words, two different inputs cannot give the same output.

We can sketch the concept of one–one as shown in Figure 4.4
   The function

$f : R \rightarrow R \quad f(x) = x^3$

is another example of a one–one function.

> A function whose range is equal to its codomain is an 'onto' function or 'surjective' function.

We can sketch the concept of onto as shown in Figure 4.5.

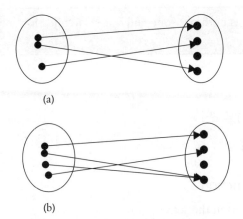

(a)

(b)

Figure 4.4   A diagram of (a) one–one function and (b) not one–one function.

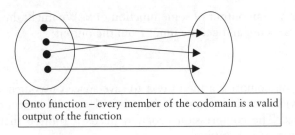

Onto function – every member of the codomain is a valid
output of the function

Figure 4.5   A diagram of an onto function.

The function

$$f : \mathsf{R} \to \mathsf{R} \qquad f(x) = x^3$$

is onto.

Example 4.14

Which of the following functions is one–one or onto or both?

1. $f : S \to T$ with $S = \{5, 6, 7\}$ and $T = \{9, 2, 1, 5\}$ and $f = \{(5, 9), (6, 1), (7, 1)\}$
2. $f : S \to T$ with $S = \{5, 6, 7\}$ and $T = \{9, 2, 1, 5\}$ and $f = \{(5, 9), (6, 1), (7, 5)\}$
3. $f : S \to T$ with $S = \{5, 6, 7\}$ and $T = \{9, 2, 1\}$ and $f = \{(5, 9), (6, 1), (7, 2)\}$

Solutions
1. Not one–one because 1 appears twice as a second argument (output) in a pair. It
   is not onto because 2 and 5 from the codomain do not appear as a second
   argument in any pair.
2. One–one.
3. One–one and onto.

> A function that is both one–one and onto is a 'bijection' or 'bijective'
> function.

The function

$$f : \mathsf{R} \rightarrow \mathsf{R} \quad f(x) = x^3$$

is a bijective function.

The inverse of a function

We have used functions in the sense

$$y = f(x)$$

which means that y is an output of some function of x. We might, however, want to
work in the reverse sense and get the input from the output:

$$y = f(x)$$

For example, if you compress a file of text to save space on your hard disk then at
some stage you will want to decompress the text and you will expect to get all of the
original text back. The compression program needs a routine that performs the
inverse of the compression routine.

> The reverse of a function is its 'inverse'. For a function f we denote its
> inverse as f^{-1}.

Example 4.15

Write down the inverse of the function

$$\{(1, 3), (7, 8), (2, 4)\}$$

Solution
To get the inverse we need to reverse the pairs

$$\{(3, 1), (8, 7), (4, 2)\}$$

For a function to be inverted it must be bijective. The need for the function to be
bijective is intuitive if you remember two basic rules about functions:

1. Any member of the domain can serve as an input.

2. An input cannot give two different outputs; in other words, a member of the
   domain cannot appear as the first argument in more than one ordered pair in the
   function set.

When a function is inverted the codomain and domain are swapped because we have the reverse mapping:

$$f : S \to T$$
$$f^{-1} : T \to S$$

We saw in Example 4.14 that the function

$$f : S \to T \text{ with } S = \{5, 6, 7\} \text{ and } T = \{9, 2, 1, 5\} \text{ and } f = \{(5, 9), (6, 1), (7, 1)\}$$

is not one–one. If we listed the pairs in reverse order we get

$$\{(9, 5), (1, 6), (1, 7)\}$$

The above pairs are not a valid function because the value 1 appears twice as the first argument in an ordered pair.

If a function is not onto then the range does not equal the codomain and this means that there will be at least one member (possibly more) which never appears as an output of the function. Therefore since we have an object in the codomain that never appears as an output of the function how can we find its input?

?

4.3

Answers appear in Appendix A.

1 Which of the following is a function?

(a) $f : S \to T$ with $S = \{a, b, c\}$ and $T = \{1, 2, 3\}$ and $f = \{(a, 3), (b, 2), (c, 1)\}$

(b) $f : S \to T$ with $S = \{a, b, c\}$ and $T = \{1, 2, 3\}$ and $f = \{(a, 1), (a, 2), (c, 3)\}$

(c) $f : S \to T$ with $S = \{a, b, c\}$ and $T = \{1, 2, 3\}$ and $f = \{(a, 1), (c, 3), (b, 3)\}$

(d) $f : S \to T$ with $S = \{a, b, c\}$ and $T = \{1, 2, 3\}$ and $f = \{(a, 1), (c, 3), (b, 4)\}$

(e) $f : S \to T$ with $S = \{a, b, c\}$ and $T = \{1, 2, 3\}$ and $f = \{(a, 1), (c, 1), (b, 1)\}$

2 For each of the following functions, state whether the function is
one–one
onto
bijective

(a) $f : S \to T$ with $S = \{a, b, c\}$ and $T = \{1, 2, 3\}$ and $f = \{(a, 3), (b, 2), (c, 1)\}$

(b) $f : I \to V$ with $I = \{$Sara, John, Dave$\}$ and $V = \{100, 010, 011\}$ and $f = \{($Sara, 100), (John, 011), (Dave, 100)$\}$

(c) $f : Z \to Z$ $f(x) = x + 1$

(d) $f : R \to R$ $f(x) = 3x + 4$

Composition of functions

Suppose we have the functions:

$$f: R \rightarrow R \quad f(x) = x^3$$

$$g: R \rightarrow R \quad g(x) = x + 3$$

and suppose that we apply the function f first and then take the output of f as input to g. The result of applying f followed by g can be written as a new function h

$$h: R \rightarrow R \quad h(x) = x^3 + 3$$

We see that h is the 'composition' of g with f and is written as

$$h(x) = (g \circ f)(x) \quad \text{or}$$

$$h(x) = g(f(x))$$

Programmers use procedure composition in a natural way to structure code; it is good practice to structure programs into small procedures (routines) where the program flows with output from one procedure serving as input to the next. Just as with computer programs the order of composition matters. For example,

$$h(3) = 3^3 + 3 = 30$$

but if we define h as

$$h(x) = (f \circ g)(x)$$

we get

$$h(3) = (3 + 3)^3 = 216$$

?

4.4

Answers appear in Appendix A.

1 Given that

$$f: R \rightarrow R \qquad f(x) = -x$$

$$g: R \rightarrow R \qquad g(x) = x + 5$$

$$h(x) = (g \circ f)(x)$$

$$j(x) = (f \circ g)(x)$$

Evaluate
(a) $h(-3)$
(b) $h(4)$
(c) $j(-3)$
(d) $j(4)$

2 Given

$f = \{(\text{brain}, \text{ain}), (\text{transport}, \text{ort}), (\text{park}, \text{ark})\}$

$g = \{(\text{ain}, \text{nia}), (\text{ort}, \text{tro}), (\text{ark}, \text{kra})\}$

define $h(x) = (g \circ f)(x)$

Partial functions

If the domain of a function contains objects that are not to serve as inputs to a function then the function is a 'partial function'. Partial functions are very common in computing. For example, you might have a function that expects an integer value to be typed by the user but the function will only operate on the values $\{1, 2, 3, 4, 5\}$. So the domain is the set of integers but the valid inputs are restricted to $\{1, 2, 3, 4, 5\}$. We can turn the function into a 'total function' by specifying a precondition. The precondition in this example states that the domain is

$\{1, 2, 3, 4, 5\}$ or alternatively

$\{x \mid x \in \mathbb{N} \wedge 1 \leq x \leq 5\}$

The function that gives the square root of a number is a partial function on the set of real numbers; you cannot take the square root of a negative number. We can define the square root as a total function by setting a precondition on the domain

$\{x \mid x \in \mathbb{R} \wedge x > 0\}$

'Post-conditions' are sometimes used to specify the range of a function. It is good practice for developers of software libraries (a collection of software routines, e.g., for producing business charts) to specify routines with pre- and post-conditions. Using pre- and post-conditions the developer and user of the library enter into a type of contract. The developer is stating that if the user ensures that the input satisfies the preconditions then the developer will ensure that the output satisfies the post-conditions.

Summary

- A binary relation R can be represented using infix notation aRb. The relation can also be represented as a predicate that takes two objects as arguments. Another way to represent a binary relation between the two sets A and B is to list the ordered pairs in $A \times B$ that satisfy the relation.
- If a relation R on a set S is reflexive then each member x of the set S appears as an ordered pair (x,x) in $S \times S$.
- If a relation is symmetric then wherever the ordered pair (a, b) appears the pair (b, a) should also appear.
- If an object a is related to b and b is related to c it means that a is related to c then the relation is said to be transitive.

- If a relation is reflexive, symmetric and transitive, then it is an equivalence relation. The relation $m \equiv n(\mathrm{mod}\ p)$ on the set of integers is an equivalence relation.
- If for two different objects a and b we have aRb but cannot have bRa then the relation is antisymmetric. Another way of looking at this property is to say that if we find the pairs (a, b) and (b, a) as members of the relation then a must be equal to b for the relation to be antisymmetric.
- A binary relation on a set S that is reflexive, antisymmetric and transitive is called a partial ordering on S.
- A function associates each object in the domain to a unique object in the codomain. The objects that can be input to a function are members of the domain and the outputs from a function are members of the codomain. The members of the codomain that can appear as outputs of a function are members of the range.
- A function can be expressed as a mapping from the domain to codomain written as

$$f : S \to T$$

This mapping is a subset of $S \times T$ where a member of S can appear only once as the first argument of an ordered pair.
- If a distinct input always gives a distinct output then the function is one–one (one to one) or injective. In other words, two different inputs cannot give the same output.
- A function whose range is equal to its codomain is an onto function or surjective function.
- A function that is both one–one and onto is a bijection or bijective function.
- The reverse of a function is its inverse. For a function f we denote its inverse as f^{-1}. For a function to have an inverse it must be bijective.
- The composition of function g with function f is written as

$$h(x) = (g \circ f)(x) \quad \text{or}$$

$$h(x) = g(f(x))$$

EXERCISES

Answers appear in Appendix B.

1 Given the set {b, c, a} test the following relations for the properties: symmetric, antisymmetric, transitive or reflexive.
    (a) {(b, e), (a, e), (a, b)}
    (b) {(b, b), (b, e), (e, e), (a, a), (a, b), (a, e), (c, c)}

2 Given the set {1, 2, 3} test the following relations for the properties: symmetric, antisymmetric, transitive or reflexive.
    (a) {(1, 3), (2, 2), (3, 1)}
    (b) {(3, 1), (3, 2), (2, 1)}
    (c) {(1, 1), (1, 3), (3, 1), (3, 3)}
    (d) {(1, 1), (2, 2), (3, 3), (1, 2), (2, 1)}

3 State whether the relation '$x + y$ is even' on the set of integers is symmetric, antisymmetric, transitive or reflexive.

4 Define the relation *same-sex-as* on the set {Jane, David, Sara, Peter, John} in terms of the union of set products.

5 For the function {(1, 1), (2, 8), (−1, −1), (−2, −8)} list the set of objects for the domain and codomain.

6 Give the set of ordered pairs satisfying

$$\{(x, f(x)) \mid f(x) = x^2 \wedge x \in N \wedge 2 < x < 8\}$$

7 State which of the following are valid functions
   (a) $f: S \rightarrow T$ $S = \{$rob, Dave, Mark$\}$ $T = N$
        $f = \{($rob, 190$), ($Dave, 185$), ($Mark, 187$)\}$
   (b) $f: S \rightarrow T$ $S = \{-2, -1, 0, 1, 2, 3\}$ $T = \{4, 1, 0, 9, 36, 16\}$
        $f = \{(-2, 4), (-1, 1), (0, 0), (1, 1), (2, 4), (3, 9)\}$
   (c) $f: S \rightarrow T$ $S = \{-2, -1, 0, 1, 2, 3\}$ $T = \{4, 1, 0, 9, 36, 16\}$
        $f = \{(-2, 4), (-1, 1), (0, 0), (1, 1), (2, 4), (3, 9), (2, 3)\}$

8 For each of the following functions state whether it is one–one, onto or bijective.
   (a) $f: S \rightarrow T$ $S = \{abde, gh, ijkhy, ght\}$ $T = \{0, 1, 2, 3, 4, 5\}$
        $f = \{(abde, 4), (gh, 2), (ijkhy, 5), (ght, 3)\}$
   (b) $f: S \rightarrow T$ $S = \{abde, gh, ijkhy, ght, jkh\}$ $T = \{2, 3, 4, 5\}$
        $f = \{(abde, 4), (gh, 2), (ijkhy, 5), (ght, 3), (jkh, 3)\}$
   (c) $f: S \rightarrow T$ $S = \{abde, gh, ijkhy, ght\}$ $T = \{2, 3, 4, 5\}$
        $f = \{(abde, 4), (gh, 2), (ijkhy, 5), (ght, 3)\}$
   (d) $f: S \rightarrow T$ $S = \{000, 001, 010, 011, 100, 101, 110, 111\}$ $T = \{0, 1, 2, 3, 4, 5, 6, 7, 8\}$
        $f = \{(000, 0), (001, 1), (010, 2), (011, 3), (100, 4), (101, 5), (110, 6), (111, 7)\}$
   (e) Domain = words in a dictionary, Codomain = any string of characters
        f = reverse of characters (e.g., BRAIN becomes NIARB)

9 Given the function $f: N \rightarrow N$ $f(x) = 4x + 2$ describe f^{-1}.

10 Given $f: N \rightarrow N$ $f(x) = 4x + 2$ and $g: N \rightarrow N$ $g(x) = 2x$
   (a) evaluate $(g \circ f)(3)$
   (b) evaluate $(f \circ g)(3)$
   (c) evaluate $(f \circ f)(3)$
   (d) evaluate $(g \circ f)(x)$

5

Vectors and matrices

Introduction

Vectors and matrices are fundamental structures that are widely used by programmers to represent information and they provide the basis for allowing the implementation of fast algorithms that are essential for many applications. Much of the subject matter in this chapter falls under the mathematical topic of linear algebra. Vectors and matrices are part of the basic mathematical toolkit used routinely by engineers and scientists and since much of computing has a scientific and engineering base it is not surprising to find that linear algebra has a significant role within computing. What we call a matrix is often called an array in a computer programming text. Programming languages support arrays in one form or another. The chapter starts with an introduction to what a vector is and some basic vector operations. After introducing matrices we shall look at the way in which matrices can be used to solve sets of linear equations. Studying the solution of linear equations is a useful preparation for the study of more advanced matrix techniques that have many computing applications. The overall aim of the chapter is to introduce some topics of basic linear algebra that are a prerequisite for the study of more advanced computing techniques that have wide ranging applications. Chapter 6 continues the study of matrices with an introduction to determinants before concluding with an overview of some applications.

Vectors

We are familiar with the idea of plotting points on an x-y graph. Each point's location in the graph is given by an x-coordinate and a y-coordinate. Because each point's position is defined by two numbers (i.e., the coordinates) we say that the point is in two-dimensional space. We can also picture a point in three-dimensional space. For example, if you wish to specify the location of a point inside a cube, you can give its position as (x, y, z) coordinates. Two- and three-dimensional space is illustrated in Figure 5.1.

Strictly speaking, the space that we are talking about is known as 'Euclidean' space. Euclidean 1-space is just the set of real numbers; Euclidean 2-space is the set of all ordered pairs of real numbers and is often called the plane; Euclidean 3-space

Figure 5.1   Two- and three-dimensional coordinate
systems.

is the set of all ordered triples of real numbers (a triple is three objects written like (x, y, z)). These spaces are denoted by R for 1-space, R^2 for 2-space and R^3 for 3-space. So when dealing with points inside a cube we are dealing with a subset of R^3.

We can picture objects in two-dimensional and three-dimensional space. We can also perform operations in this space. For instance, we can measure the distance between points. What might seem strange is that we can have higher-dimensional spaces; in fact there is no limit to the number of dimensions. Although it is not possible to visualise these higher-dimensional spaces, we can perform operations like measuring the distance between points. For four dimensions, a point is described using four numbers (x, y, z, w), five dimensions needs five numbers, and so on. We need to be consistent that the numbers always appear in the same order, that is, the x-coordinate is given first, the y-coordinate second and so on. When we deal with high-dimensional spaces we are soon going to run out of letters with which to denote the coordinates. To overcome this we adopt the convention of describing each coordinate using the variable x with a subscript number that identifies whether the variable is the first, second or third, etc., coordinate. So we replace (x, y) and (x, y, z) with (x_1, x_2) and (x_1, x_2, x_3) respectively. For spaces in R^n (n-dimensional), a point is described as $(x_1, x_2, ..., x_n)$.

Normally we would show an ordered pair of numbers (x_1, x_2), or a triple (x_1, x_2, x_3), as a point. An example is shown in Figure 5.2.

Physicists have another way of interpreting these points in space. Their interpretation was motivated by the desire to mathematically represent the forces that act on a body. For example, when you push a car, the force you exert has both a magnitude (i.e., its strength) and a direction. This force can be geometrically represented as a vector. So an ordered pair of numbers can be treated as a vector. The vector would be indicated as shown in Figure 5.3.

Notice that the vector has been denoted by **v** and that the pair of numbers is now written in square brackets. There is no need to use commas to separate the numbers if the notation is clear. It is typical to denote a vector by a lower-case letter. It is convention to write the vector in bold font to distinguish it from a scalar (a scalar is a single real number).

The individual elements (numbers) that make up **v** are denoted as:

$$\mathbf{v} = [v_1, v_2, ..., v_n]$$

So, in Figure 5.3, the vector has $v_1 = 2$ and $v_2 = 3$. You can think of v_1 as a substitute for x_1 and v_2 as a substitute for x_2.

Figure 5.2   An ordered pair shown as a point.

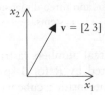

Figure 5.3   An ordered pair shown as a vector.

Vectors are normally drawn as originating from the origin, point (0, 0), but they can be drawn from another starting point in which case we say that the vector has been 'translated' (see Figure 5.4).

Vector addition

Vectors can be added and subtracted. For example, you might have two forces acting on a body and you need to find the resultant force which is a force that on its own would be equivalent to the two other forces acting together. The addition of two vectors can be depicted as in Figure 5.5.

To get the resultant vector from the addition of **v** and **w**, likewise elements are summed:

$$\mathbf{v} + \mathbf{w} = [v_1 + w_1, v_2 + w_2]$$

For two vectors of n-dimensions (i.e., n elements), the result of addition is:

$$\mathbf{v} + \mathbf{w} = [v_1 + w_1, v_2 + w_2, ..., v_n + w_n]$$

Two vectors can also be subtracted. The geometrical view of subtracting two vectors is shown in Figure 5.6.

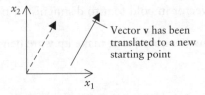

Figure 5.4   The translation of a vector results in a vector being shifted from its original position. The vector maintains the same magnitude and direction.

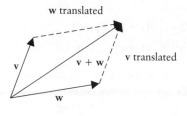

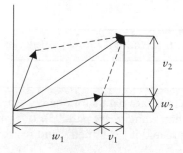

Figure 5.5 Illustration of adding two vectors **v** and **w**.

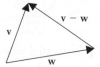

Figure 5.6 The subtraction of two vectors.

To subtract two vectors, you subtract likewise elements:

$$\mathbf{v} - \mathbf{w} = [v_1 - w_1,\, v_2 - w_2,\, \dots,\, v_n - w_n]$$

A vector can also be multiplied by a scalar as:

$$r\mathbf{v} = [rv_1,\, rv_2,\, \dots,\, rv_n]$$

Example 5.1

For the two vectors

$$\mathbf{p} = [3, 4, -2]$$
$$\mathbf{q} = [1, 5, -4]$$

1. Find **p** + **q**
2. Find **p** − **q**
3. Find the vector that is double the length of **p** and is in the same direction as **p**.

Solution

1. $p + q = [3 + 1, 4 + 5, -2 + -4] = [4, 9, -6]$

2. $p - q = [3 - 1, 4 - 5, -2 - -4] = [2, -1, 2]$

3. To obtain the vector that is in the same direction as **p** but twice its length, we multiply it by the scalar 2:

$$2p = [6, 8, -4]$$

> A vector whose elements are all 0 is known as the zero vector.

> Two *n*-dimensional vectors are parallel if one is a scalar multiple of the other (i.e., if $rv = w$ then **v** and **w** are parallel). If $r > 0$, then **v** and **w** have the same direction, and if $r < 0$ then **v** and **w** are in opposite directions.

Example 5.2

Determine if **p** is parallel to **q** and if **p** is parallel to **v** given:

$$p = [2, 4]$$
$$q = [3, 6]$$
$$v = [-2, -4]$$

Solution

If **p** is parallel to **q** then $rp = q$. So,

$$r2 = 3 \text{ and } r4 = 6$$

A solution is found with $r = 1.5$. Since the value of r is the same for each pair of elements then both vectors are parallel. The vectors are also in the same direction because $r > 0$.

Similarly for **p** and **v**

$$r2 = -2 \text{ and } r4 = -4$$

Both vectors are parallel since $r = -1$ for both pairs of elements. The vectors are in opposite directions since $r < 0$.

Magnitude and norm

> The magnitude or norm of a vector is its length. The magnitude of $\mathbf{v}$ is denoted by $\|\mathbf{v}\|$. For an n-dimensional vector the magnitude is
>
> $$\|\mathbf{v}\| = \sqrt{v_1^2 + v_2^2 + \ldots + v_n^2}$$

Example 5.3

Find the magnitude of $\mathbf{p}$ given

$\mathbf{p} = [3, 4, -2]$

Solution

$$\|\mathbf{p}\| = \sqrt{3^2 + 4^2 + -2^2} = \sqrt{29}$$

> A unit vector is a vector whose magnitude is 1. For a vector v, the unit vector is given by
>
> $$\left(\frac{1}{\|\mathbf{v}\|}\right)\mathbf{v}$$

Example 5.4

Find a unit vector having the same direction as $\mathbf{p}$.

$\mathbf{p} = [3, 4, -2]$

Solution

The norm of $\mathbf{p}$ was calculated in the previous example as 29, and so the unit vector $\mathbf{u}$ is:

$$\mathbf{u} = [3/\sqrt{29}, 4/\sqrt{29}, -2/\sqrt{29}]$$

Dot product

The dot product of two vectors gives a scalar that can be used to find the angle between two vectors (see Figure 5.7). The dot product of two vectors, $\mathbf{v}$ and $\mathbf{w}$, in n-dimensional space is given by

$$\mathbf{v} \bullet \mathbf{w} = v_1 w_1 + v_2 w_2 + \ldots + v_n w_n$$

It can be shown, using the law of cosines, that

$$\mathbf{v} \bullet \mathbf{w} = \|\mathbf{v}\|\|\mathbf{w}\|(\cos \theta)$$

From this, we can calculate the angle between two vectors as

$$\cos^{-1}\left(\frac{\mathbf{v} \bullet \mathbf{w}}{\|\mathbf{v}\|\|\mathbf{w}\|}\right)$$

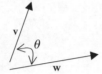

Figure 5.7   The dot product is a scalar value that shows the association between two vectors' magnitudes and directions.

The dot product is also known as the 'inner product' or 'scalar product'.

Example 5.5

Find the angle between the vectors **v** and **w**

$$\mathbf{v} = [3, 4, 6]$$
$$\mathbf{w} = [3, 7, 5]$$

Solution
The dot product is

$$\mathbf{v} \bullet \mathbf{w} = 3 \times 3 + 4 \times 7 + 6 \times 5 = 67$$

The magnitude for **v** and **w** are

$$\|\mathbf{v}\| = \sqrt{3^2 + 4^2 + 6^2} = \sqrt{61}$$
$$\|\mathbf{w}\| = \sqrt{3^2 + 7^2 + 5^2} = \sqrt{83}$$

Therefore the angle is

$$\cos^{-1} = \frac{67}{\sqrt{61}\sqrt{83}} = 19.68^0$$

Column and row vectors

All of the vectors so far in this chapter have been written as row vectors; a vector is written as a row of numbers. We can also write a vector as a column vector; a vector is written as a column of numbers. For instance,

$$v = \begin{bmatrix} 3 \\ -7 \\ 4 \\ 9 \end{bmatrix}$$

is a vector in R^4.

The 'transpose' of a row vector is the vector written as a column vector, and the transpose of a column vector is a row vector. For example, suppose **w** is the transpose of **v** written

$$w = v^T$$

$$w = [3 \ -7 \ 4 \ 9]$$

5.1

Answers appear in Appendix A.

1 Find the following for the vectors **p** and **q**

$$p = [-6 \ 4 \ 3]$$

$$q = [3 \ 1 \ 3]$$

(a) **p** + **q**

(b) **p** − **q**

(c) The vector that is double the length of **p** and is in the same direction as **p**.

(d) The magnitude of **p**

(e) The dot product of **p** with **q**

(f) The transpose of **q**

2 Repeat Question 1 with the vectors

$$p = [4 \ -2 \ 1 \ 1]$$

$$q = [6 \ -3 \ -1 \ 2]$$

Matrices

A matrix is a series of elements that make up a number of rows and columns. A vector of n-dimensions can be considered as a matrix that has either, 1 row and n-columns or n-rows and 1 column depending on which way it is written. The elements in a matrix follow a pre-specified order. The order of elements is important since the matrix will usually represent some specific set of information. For example, we might use a matrix to represent the age, height and weight of the players in a rugby team:

$$\begin{bmatrix} & age & \text{height in cm} & \text{weight in kg} \\ \text{Andrew} & 24 & 190 & 95 \\ \text{Tony} & 25 & 185 & 105 \\ \text{Dave} & 28 & 176 & 90 \\ \text{Gary} & 32 & 192 & 110 \\ & \vdots & & \end{bmatrix}$$

The players are represented by rows and their ages, heights and weights by columns. Row and column labels are not usually shown.

The size of a matrix is specified by the number of rows and the number of columns. A 4×3 matrix means that the matrix has four rows and three columns. An upper-case letter is usually used to denote a matrix. For example,

$$A = \begin{bmatrix} 24 & 190 & 95 \\ 25 & 185 & 105 \\ 28 & 176 & 90 \\ 32 & 192 & 110 \end{bmatrix}$$

The elements of a matrix are indexed using a double subscript:

$$A = \begin{bmatrix} a_{11} & a_{12} & a_{13} \ldots a_{1n} \\ a_{21} & a_{22} & a_{23} \ldots a_{2n} \\ a_{31} & a_{32} & a_{33} \ldots a_{3n} \\ \vdots \\ a_{m1} & a_{m2} & a_{m3} \ldots a_{mn} \end{bmatrix}$$

For example, for our rugby players $a_{23} = 105$ and $a_{42} = 192$.

Matrix multiplication

A matrix can be considered as being made up of a number of row vectors or alternatively as a number of column vectors. Two matrices can be multiplied by taking the dot product of every row in the first matrix, with every column in the second matrix. To get the dot product, the number of elements in each vector must match; therefore to perform multiplication, the number of columns in the first matrix must match the number of rows in the second matrix. Also, the size of the matrix that results from the multiplication will contain a number of elements that is equal to the number of dot products taken; the resultant matrix will have the same number of rows as the first matrix and the same number of columns as the second matrix.

Example 5.6

The matrix C, is the product of A and B. Find C.

$$C = AB = \begin{bmatrix} 3 & 2 & 8 \\ -2 & 5 & 6 \\ 1 & -4 & 2 \end{bmatrix} \begin{bmatrix} 5 & 9 \\ 2 & 4 \\ 3 & 6 \end{bmatrix} = \begin{bmatrix} 43 & 83 \\ 18 & 38 \\ 3 & 5 \end{bmatrix}$$

Solution
The first element of the first row is calculated by taking the dot product of the first row in A with the first column in B:

$$[3 \ 2 \ 8] \begin{bmatrix} 5 \\ 2 \\ 3 \end{bmatrix} = 43 \quad \text{i.e., } 3 \times 5 + 2 \times 2 + 8 \times 3 = 43$$

The second element of the first row is calculated by taking the dot product of the first row in A with the second column in B:

$$[3 \quad 2 \quad 8] \begin{bmatrix} 9 \\ 4 \\ 6 \end{bmatrix} = 83$$

The second row of elements is found by taking the product of the second row in A with both column vectors of B in turn. The third row of elements is found by taking the product of the third row in A with both column vectors of B in turn.

> Let A be an $m \times n$ matrix and B an $n \times s$. The matrix product $C = AB$ is an $m \times s$ matrix where the element c_{ij} is the dot product of the ith row of A with the jth column of B.

It is important to realise that matrix multiplication is not commutative which means that AB need not equal BA (assuming of course both AB and BA can be calculated). The element c_{ij} can be defined using the summation notation:

$$c_{ij} = a_{i1}b_{1j} + a_{i2}b_{2j} + \ldots + a_{in}b_{nj}$$

$$= \sum_{k=1}^{n} a_{ik}b_{kj}$$

So, to calculate the first element in the first row of C, i and j are both 1 and k varies from 1 to n:

$$c_{11} = a_{11}b_{11} + a_{12}b_{21} + \ldots + a_{1n}b_{n1}$$

Identity matrix

> A 'square' matrix is a matrix with an equal number of rows and columns: a square matrix is an $n \times n$ matrix.

> The 'identity' matrix is a square matrix with all elements having a value of 0 apart from the diagonal elements whose values are set to 1. Let I be $n \times n$ identity matrix. Then an element a of I has:
>
> $$a_{ij} \begin{cases} 1 \; if \; i = j \\ 0 \; if \; i \neq j \end{cases}$$

So, the identity matrix for $n = 4$ is:

$$I = \begin{bmatrix} 1 & 0 & 0 & 0 \\ 0 & 1 & 0 & 0 \\ 0 & 0 & 1 & 0 \\ 0 & 0 & 0 & 1 \end{bmatrix}$$

If we multiply a scalar value by 1 then we get the scalar value. For example, 3 multiplied by 1 is 3. The identity matrix behaves in a similar way for matrices since:

$$AI = A$$

$$IA = A$$

Adding matrices

Two matrices of the same size (i.e., same number of rows and columns in each matrix) can be added by summing like elements:

$$c_{ij} = a_{ij} + b_{ij}$$

A matrix can also be multiplied by a scalar r. If $B = rA$:

$$b_{ij} = ra_{ij}$$

Example 5.7

$$A = \begin{bmatrix} 2 & 6 & 3 \\ 5 & 3 & -2 \end{bmatrix}$$

$$B = \begin{bmatrix} 4 & 8 & 3 \\ 7 & -5 & 7 \end{bmatrix}$$

For matrices A and B, find

(a) $A + B$

(b) $2A$

Solution

(a) $A + B = \begin{bmatrix} 6 & 14 & 6 \\ 12 & -2 & 5 \end{bmatrix}$

(b) $2A = \begin{bmatrix} 4 & 12 & 6 \\ 10 & 6 & -4 \end{bmatrix}$

Transpose of a matrix and symmetric matrices

> The transpose of a matrix changes a row vector to a column vector or vice versa. A matrix B is the transpose of A, written A^T, if $b_{ij} = a_{ji}$.
>
> A symmetric matrix is the same as its transpose:
>
> $$A = A^T$$

Example 5.8

$$A = \begin{bmatrix} 2 & 6 & 3 \\ 5 & 3 & -2 \end{bmatrix}$$

$$B = \begin{bmatrix} 2 & 6 & 3 \\ 6 & 3 & -2 \\ 3 & -2 & 4 \end{bmatrix}$$

Find the transpose of A and the transpose of B

Solution

$$A^T = \begin{bmatrix} 2 & 5 \\ 6 & 3 \\ 3 & -2 \end{bmatrix}$$

$$B^T = \begin{bmatrix} 2 & 6 & 3 \\ 6 & 3 & -2 \\ 3 & -2 & 4 \end{bmatrix}$$

?

5.2

Answers appear in Appendix A.

1 For the following matrices

$$A = \begin{bmatrix} 4 & 6 & 5 \\ 1 & -3 & 2 \end{bmatrix}$$

$$B = \begin{bmatrix} -1 & 1 & 2 \\ -3 & 2 & 4 \\ 5 & 2 & 6 \end{bmatrix}$$

(a) Give a_{23}

(b) $A + A$

(c) The product AB

(d) The transpose of B

(e) The product AA^T

Solving linear equations

Many problems require a set of linear equations to be solved. Consider a linear equation in two unknowns:

$$y = 3x - 2$$

This is the equation of a straight line with a slope of 3 and intercept of -2 as shown in Figure 5.8. The solution set, which is any pair of numbers (x, y) that satisfy the equation, is the straight line. For any pair of numbers to be a solution, the value of x must give the value of y when substituted into the equation. For example, $(2, 4)$ is a solution since:

$$4 = 3 \times 2 - 2$$

Note also, that with some rearranging, we can write the above equation as

$$3x - y = 2$$

Two lines will usually intersect at some point as illustrated in Figure 5.9. The solution to the two straight line equations is the point of interception. For example, the two lines

$$x - 2y = 3$$
$$x + y = 6$$

intercept at $(5, 1)$. We can check this by substituting for $x = 5$ and $y = 1$ into the above equations:

$$5 - 2 \times 1 = 3$$
$$5 + 1 = 6$$

The point $(5, 1)$ is the solution since substitution in the first equation gives 3 and in the second gives 6.

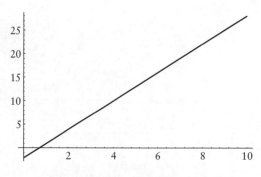

Figure 5.8   Plot of the line $y = 3x - 2$.

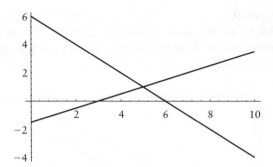

Figure 5.9   The intersection of the two lines is the solution to the two straight line
equations $x - 2y = 3$ and $x + y = 6$.

The solution to the above equations can be found by cancelling one of the
unknowns (i.e., x or y) and solving for the other. To cancel an unknown, you
multiply one of the equations by a factor such that when the equations are added
together, the unknown is cancelled. Once a solution for one unknown is found, the
other can be found by substitution.

Example 5.9

Find the solution to the two equations given below.

$$x - 2y = 3 \qquad\qquad (1)$$
$$x + y = 6 \qquad\qquad (2)$$

Solution
Multiply (1) by -1 and add the two equations

$$-x + 2y = -3$$
$$\underline{x + y = 6}$$
$$3y = 3$$

So $y = 1$. The value for x can be found by substituting y back into either equation.
Substituting back into (1)

$$x - 2 \times 1 = 3$$

which gives $x = 5$.

Two equations that are parallel like that shown in Figure 5.10 have no solution.
Two lines that are coincident (i.e., have the same slope and intercept) have an infinite
number of solutions. It is highly likely, that any two lines chosen at random will
intersect at some point. Because we can draw any number of lines to intersect at a

common point, it is possible to have 100 or more straight line equations with a single solution. We have said that two lines are likely to intersect. We can extend this to a plane (a plane is an equation in three unknowns). Three planes are likely to intersect. We can extend our method for solving two equations in two unknowns to three equations in three unknowns.

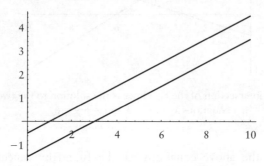

Figure 5.10   Two parallel equations.

Example 5.10

Find the solution to the set of equations

$$2x + y - 2z = 7 \qquad (1)$$

$$3x + 2y + z = 7 \qquad (2)$$

$$x + 3y + z = 4 \qquad (3)$$

Solution
We can eliminate x from (1) by multiplying (3) by -2 and adding to (1):

$$-5y - 4z = -1 \qquad (1)$$

$$3x + 2y + z = 7 \qquad (2)$$

$$x + 3y + z = 4 \qquad (3)$$

We can now eliminate x from (2) by multiplying (3) by -3 and adding to (2):

$$-5y - 4z = -1 \qquad (1)$$

$$-7y + -2z = -5 \qquad (2)$$

$$x + 3y + z = 4 \qquad (3)$$

We can now eliminate z from (1) by multiplying (2) by -2 and adding to (1):

$$9y = 9 \qquad (1)$$

$$-7y + -2z = -5 \qquad (2)$$

$$x + 3y + z = 4 \qquad (3)$$

From (1) we get that $y = 1$. Substituting back into (2) for y we get

$$-7 + -2z = -5$$
$$-2z = 2$$
$$z = -1$$

And finally, substituting for y and z into (3) we get

$$x + 3 + -1 = 4$$
$$x = 2$$

We can check the result by substituting for x, y, and z into the original equations.

We have proceeded to solve our equations by multiplying an equation by some scalar and adding two equations to cancel a term. We shall explore in a later section a matrix method for solving sets of linear equations and it will be seen that this method relies on basic row manipulation that involves multiplying by scalars and adding one row to another.

Matrix representation of a system of linear equations

Computers solve systems of linear equations by performing matrix manipulations. Because we might need to handle a set of equations in many unknowns it is more convenient to denote a variable (i.e., unknown) using the notation $x_1, x_2, \ldots x_n$. A set of equations can then be expressed in the following notation:

$$a_{11}x_1 + a_{12}x_2 + \ldots a_{1n}x_n = b_1$$
$$a_{21}x_1 + a_{22}x_2 + \ldots a_{2n}x_n = b_2$$
$$\vdots$$
$$a_{m1}x_1 + a_{m2}x_2 + \ldots a_{mn}x_n = b_m$$

The above set of equations can be written as

$$A\mathbf{x} = \mathbf{b}$$

The matrix A contains all of the coefficients a_{ij}. The column vector $\mathbf{x}$ is each unknown, $x_1, x_2, \ldots x_n$, and the column vector $\mathbf{b}$ contains the components b_i.

Example 5.11

Write the following equations in the form $A\mathbf{x} = \mathbf{b}$

$$2x_1 + x_2 - 2x_3 = 7 \quad (1)$$
$$3x_1 + 2x_2 + x_3 = 7 \quad (2)$$
$$x_1 + 3x_2 + x_3 = 4 \quad (3)$$

Solution

$$\begin{bmatrix} 2 & 1 & -2 \\ 3 & 2 & 1 \\ 1 & 3 & 1 \end{bmatrix} \begin{bmatrix} x_1 \\ x_2 \\ x_3 \end{bmatrix} = \begin{bmatrix} 7 \\ 7 \\ 4 \end{bmatrix}$$

We can also form a compact representation known as the 'augmented' matrix or 'partitioned' matrix:

$$\begin{bmatrix} a_{11} & a_{12} & \dots & a_{1n} & b_1 \\ a_{21} & a_{22} & \dots & a_{2n} & b_2 \\ & \vdots & & & \vdots \\ a_{m1} & a_{m2} & & a_{mn} & b_m \end{bmatrix}$$

$$\begin{bmatrix} 2 & 1 & -2 & 7 \\ 3 & 2 & 1 & 7 \\ 1 & 3 & 1 & 4 \end{bmatrix}$$

Gauss method with back substitution for solving a set of linear equations

In this section we present a matrix procedure for solving a set of linear equations. The procedure is known as Gauss reduction with back substitution. The procedure requires that we form an augmented matrix and then reduce this matrix to a 'row-echelon form'.

A matrix is in row-echelon form if

1. A row containing nonzero entries appears above a row containing only zeros.

2. The first nonzero entry in a row appears in a column to the right of the first nonzero entry in the row above.

Example 5.12

Which of the following matrices is in row-echelon form?

$$A = \begin{bmatrix} 3 & 5 & 3 \\ 4 & 0 & 0 \\ 0 & 0 & 0 \end{bmatrix} \quad B = \begin{bmatrix} 0 & 5 & 3 \\ 3 & 0 & 0 \\ 0 & 0 & 0 \end{bmatrix} \quad C = \begin{bmatrix} 6 & 4 & 2 \\ 0 & 2 & 3 \\ 0 & 0 & 0 \end{bmatrix} \quad D = \begin{bmatrix} 6 & 4 & 2 \\ 0 & 2 & 3 \\ 0 & 0 & 1 \end{bmatrix}$$

$$E = \begin{bmatrix} 0 & 6 & 3 & 1 \\ 0 & 0 & 4 & 0 \\ 0 & 0 & 0 & 0 \\ 0 & 0 & 0 & 0 \end{bmatrix}$$

Solution

A is not in row-echelon form because the first nonzero entry in row two is not to the right of the first nonzero entry in row one. B is not in row-echelon form for the same reason that A is not. C is in row echelon form; the row with zero entries appears below the other two rows and the first nonzero entry in row two is to the right of the first nonzero entry in row one. D is in row-echelon form; all of the first nonzero entries appear to the right of the first nonzero entry of the preceding row (the row above). Finally E is in row-echelon form.

Now that we know what it means for a matrix to be in row-echelon form, we need a procedure for getting a matrix into row-echelon form.

Procedure to get a matrix into row-echelon form

1. Identify the first leftmost column with a nonzero entry: in other words, we ignore the first column if all of its entries are zero, and the next column if all of its entries are zero, and so on until we find a column with a nonzero entry.

2. For the matrix that remains after step 1, we need a nonzero entry in the first column of the top row. This first nonzero entry is called the 'pivot'. We can obtain this first nonzero entry by swapping two rows if necessary. Once we have a pivot in the top row, we need to make sure that the first entry in every row below is zero. We can make the first entry zero by adding a fraction of the top row to a row below. So, if the first nonzero entry in the top row is p (the pivot) and the entry in a row below is r, if we add $-\dfrac{r}{p}$ of the top row to the row below, the row below will now have a zero entry.

3. We then cross off the column we have just worked with and the pivot row and go back to step 1.

Example 5.13

Reduce A to row-echelon form.

$$A = \begin{bmatrix} 2 & 1 & -2 \\ 3 & 2 & 1 \\ 1 & 3 & 1 \end{bmatrix}$$

Solution

Step 1. The first column has nonzero entries and so the column cannot be ignored.

Step 2. There is a nonzero entry in the first column of the top row and its value is 2. So 2 is the pivot and we want zero entries in the first column of the two rows below. We have $p = 2$ and for the second row $r = 3$. Therefore, to reduce the second row we multiply the top row by $-3/2$ and add it to row 2 to give:

$$A = \begin{bmatrix} 2 & 1 & -2 \\ 0 & 0.5 & 4 \\ 1 & 3 & 1 \end{bmatrix} \quad -3/2 \text{ times row 1 added to row 2}$$

For row 3, $r = 1$ and so to obtain a zero entry we multiply the top row by $-1/2$ and add it to the third row.

$$A = \begin{bmatrix} 2 & 1 & -2 \\ 0 & 0.5 & 4 \\ 0 & 2.5 & 2 \end{bmatrix} \quad -1/2 \text{ times row 1 added to row 3}$$

Back to Step 1. We have now finished with column 1 and so we mentally ignore it. We also ignore the row whose pivot we have worked with (i.e., the first row).

$$A = \begin{bmatrix} 2 & 1 & -2 \\ 0 & 0.5 & 4 \\ 0 & 2.5 & 2 \end{bmatrix}$$

There are nonzero entries in the leftmost column of the reduced matrix.

Step 2. The pivot of the topmost row of the reduced matrix is 0.5. We now need to make the first entry on the row below zero. So, $p = 0.5$ and $r = 2.5$, and therefore we add $-2.5/0.5$ times the top row to the one below:

$$A = \begin{bmatrix} 2 & 1 & -2 \\ 0 & 0.5 & 4 \\ 0 & 0 & -18 \end{bmatrix} \quad -2.5/0.5 \text{ times row 1 added to row 3}$$

The matrix is now in row-echelon form.

   'Back substitution' is the final stage of solving a set of equations once the matrix is in row-echelon form. The procedure is more easily explained using an example.

Example 5.14

Use Gauss reduction with back substitution to solve the following set of equations:

$$2x_1 + x_2 - 2x_3 = 7 \quad (1)$$
$$3x_1 + 2x_2 + x_3 = 7 \quad (2)$$
$$x_1 + 3x_2 + x_3 = 4 \quad (3)$$

Solution
We have already seen in Example 5.10 that the augmented matrix is:

$$\begin{bmatrix} 2 & 1 & -2 & | & 7 \\ 3 & 2 & 1 & | & 7 \\ 1 & 3 & 1 & | & 4 \end{bmatrix}$$

We now need to get the matrix into row-echelon form. The procedure follows the previous example:

$$\left[\begin{array}{ccc|c} 2 & 1 & -2 & 7 \\ 0 & 0.5 & 4 & -3.5 \\ 0 & 2.5 & 2 & 0.5 \end{array}\right] \begin{array}{l} R_2 \rightarrow -3/2R_1 + R_2 \\ R_3 \rightarrow -1/2R_1 + R_3 \end{array}$$

Note that the shorthand notation

$$R_2 \rightarrow -3/2R_1 + R_2$$

simply means that row two is transformed by adding $-3/2$ times row one to row two. It keeps the arithmetic simple if we work in whole numbers and so we will multiply rows 2 and 3 by suitable factors:

$$\left[\begin{array}{ccc|c} 2 & 1 & -2 & 7 \\ 0 & 1 & 8 & -7 \\ 0 & 5 & 4 & 1 \end{array}\right] \begin{array}{l} R_2 \rightarrow 2R_2 \\ R_3 \rightarrow 2R_3 \end{array}$$

Proceeding to the next step

$$\left[\begin{array}{ccc|c} 2 & 1 & -2 & 7 \\ 0 & 1 & 8 & -7 \\ 0 & 0 & -36 & 36 \end{array}\right] R_3 \rightarrow -5R_2 + R_3$$

The matrix is now in row-echelon form and so the final step is to use back substitution. Recall that the first column gives the entries for x_1, the second for x_2 and the third for x_3. From the row-echelon form our equations are now:

$$2x_1 + x_2 - 2x_3 = 7 \qquad (1)$$
$$x_2 + 8x_3 = 7 \qquad (2)$$
$$-36x_3 = 36 \qquad (3)$$

For equation (3) we get $x_3 = -1$. If we substitute for x_3 into equation (2) we can find x_2:

$$x_2 + 8 \times -1 = -7$$
$$x_2 = 1$$

Finally we can substitute x_2 and x_3 back into equation (1) to find x_1:

$$2x_1 + 1 - (2 \times -1) = 7$$
$$2x_1 = 4$$
$$x_1 = 2$$

Example 5.15

Use Gauss reduction with back substitution to solve the following set of equations:

$$3x_2 - x_3 = 13 \qquad (1)$$
$$x_1 + x_2 + 2x_3 = -4 \qquad (2)$$
$$-2x_1 + 2x_2 + x_3 = 0 \qquad (3)$$

Solution
The augmented matrix is:

$$\left[\begin{array}{ccc|c} 0 & 3 & -1 & 13 \\ 1 & 1 & 2 & -4 \\ -2 & 2 & 1 & 0 \end{array} \right]$$

The first column contains nonzero entries but the top row's first entry is zero and we shall interchange rows 1 and 2:

$$\left[\begin{array}{ccc|c} 1 & 1 & 2 & -4 \\ 0 & 3 & -1 & 13 \\ -2 & 2 & 1 & 0 \end{array} \right]$$

$$\left[\begin{array}{ccc|c} 1 & 1 & 2 & -4 \\ 0 & 3 & -1 & 13 \\ 0 & 4 & 5 & -8 \end{array} \right] \quad R_3 \to 2R_1 + R_3$$

$$\left[\begin{array}{ccc|c} 1 & 1 & 2 & -4 \\ 0 & 3 & -1 & 13 \\ 0 & 0 & 19 & -76 \end{array} \right] \quad R_3 \to 3(-4/3R_2 + R_3)$$

$$\left[\begin{array}{ccc|c} 1 & 1 & 2 & -4 \\ 0 & 3 & -1 & 13 \\ 0 & 0 & 1 & -4 \end{array} \right] \quad R_3 \to 1/19R_3$$

Using back substitution we find

$$x_3 = -4$$
$$x_2 = 3$$
$$x_1 = 1$$

5.3

Answers appear in Appendix A.

1 Reduce the matrix A to row-echelon form and then solve for x_1, x_2 and x_3.

$$A = \begin{bmatrix} 3 & 1 & -1 & 2 \\ 1 & 2 & 1 & 8 \\ 1 & 2 & 3 & 4 \end{bmatrix}$$

$$3x_1 + x_2 - x_3 = 2$$

$$x_1 + 2x_2 + x_3 = 8$$

$$x_1 + 2x_2 + 3x_3 = 4$$

Summary

- A vector has both magnitude and direction. For spaces in R^n (n-dimensional), the individual elements (numbers) that make up a vector $\mathbf{v}$ are denoted as:

  $$\mathbf{v} = [v_1, v_2, \dots v_n]$$

- For two vectors $\mathbf{v}$ and $\mathbf{w}$ of n-dimensions (i.e., n-elements), the result of addition is:

  $$\mathbf{v} + \mathbf{w} = [v_1 + w_1, v_2 + w_2, \dots, v_n + w_n]$$

- A vector can also be multiplied by a scalar r:

  $$r\mathbf{v} = [rv_1, rv_2, \dots, rv_n]$$

- A vector whose elements are all 0 is known as the zero vector.

- Two n-dimensional vectors are parallel if one is a scalar multiple of the other (i.e., if $r\mathbf{v} = \mathbf{w}$ then $\mathbf{v}$ and $\mathbf{w}$ are parallel). If $r > 0$, then $\mathbf{v}$ and $\mathbf{w}$ have the same direction, and if $r < 0$ then $\mathbf{v}$ and $\mathbf{w}$ are in opposite directions.

- The magnitude or norm of a vector is its length. The magnitude of $\mathbf{v}$ is denoted by $\|\mathbf{v}\|$. For an n-dimensional vector the magnitude is

  $$\|\mathbf{v}\| = \sqrt{v_1^2 + v_2^2 + \dots v_n^2}$$

- A unit vector is a vector whose magnitude is 1. For a vector $\mathbf{v}$, the unit vector is given by

  $$\left(\frac{1}{\|\mathbf{v}\|}\right)\mathbf{v}$$

- The dot product of two vectors gives a scalar that can be used to find the angle between two vectors (see Figure 5.7). The dot product of two vectors, $\mathbf{v}$ and $\mathbf{w}$, in n-dimensional space is given by

  $$\mathbf{v} \bullet \mathbf{w} = v_1 w_1 + v_2 w_2 + \dots + v_n w_n$$

- It can be shown, using the law of cosines, that

  $\mathbf{v} \bullet \mathbf{w} = \| \mathbf{v} \| \| \mathbf{w} \| (\cos \theta).$

- From this, we can calculate the angle between two vectors as

  $\cos^{-1}\left(\dfrac{\mathbf{v} \bullet \mathbf{w}}{\| \mathbf{v} \| \| \mathbf{w} \|} \right)$

- The dot product is also known as the inner product or scalar product.

- The transpose of a column vector gives a row vector and transpose of a row vector gives a column vector. If a vector $\mathbf{w}$ is the transpose of $\mathbf{v}$ we write

  $\mathbf{w} = \mathbf{v}^T$

- The elements of a matrix are indexed using a double subscript:

$$A = \begin{bmatrix} a_{11} & a_{12} & a_{13} \dots a_{1n} \\ a_{21} & a_{22} & a_{23} \dots a_{2n} \\ a_{31} & a_{32} & a_{33} \dots a_{31n} \\ & \vdots & \\ a_{m1} & a_{m2} & a_{m3} \dots a_{mn} \end{bmatrix}$$

- Let A be an $m \times n$ matrix and B an $n \times s$. The matrix product $C = AB$ is an $m \times s$ matrix where the element c_{ij} is the dot product of the ith row of A with the jth column of B.

- A square matrix is a matrix with an equal number of rows and columns: a square matrix is an $n \times n$ matrix.

- The identity matrix is a square matrix with all elements having a value of 0 apart from the diagonal elements whose values are set to 1. Let I be $n \times n$ identity matrix. Then an element a of I has:

  $a_{ij} \begin{cases} 1 \ if \ i = j \\ 0 \ if \ i \neq j \end{cases}$

- The transpose of a matrix changes a row vector to a column vector or vice versa. A matrix B is the transpose of A, written A^T, if $b_{ij} = a_{ji}$.

- A symmetric matrix is the same as its transpose:

  $A = A^T$

- The set of equations:

  $a_{11}x_1 + a_{12}x_2 + \dots a_{1n}x_n = b_1$

  $a_{21}x_1 + a_{22}x_2 + \dots a_{2n}x_n = b_2$

  $\vdots$

  $a_{m1}x_1 + a_{m2}x_2 + \dots a_{mn}x_n = b_m$

can be represented by the augmented matrix or partitioned matrix:

$$\begin{bmatrix} a_{11} & a_{12} \dots & a_{1n} \big| b_1 \\ a_{21} & a_{22} \dots & a_{2n} \big| b_2 \\ & \vdots & \vdots \\ a_{m1} & & a_{mn} \big| b_m \end{bmatrix}$$

- A matrix is in row-echelon form if:

1. A row containing nonzero entries appears above a row containing only zeros.
2. The first nonzero entry in a row appears in a column to the right of the first nonzero entry in the row above.

- Procedure to get a matrix into row-echelon form

1. Identify the first leftmost column with a nonzero entry: in other words, we ignore the first column if all of its entries are zero, and the next column if all of its entries are zero, and so on until we find a column with a nonzero entry.

2. For the matrix that remains after step 1, we need a nonzero entry in the first column of the top row. This first nonzero entry is called the pivot. We can obtain this first nonzero entry by swapping two rows if necessary. Once we have a pivot in the top row, we need to make sure that the first entry in every row below is zero. We can make the first entry zero by adding a fraction of the top row to a row below. So, if the first nonzero entry in the top row is p (the pivot) and the entry in a row below is r, if we add $-\dfrac{r}{p}$ of the top row to the row below, the row below will now have a zero entry.

3. We then cross-off the column we have just worked with and the pivot row and go back to step 1.

EXERCISES

Answers appear in Appendix B.

1 Let

$$\mathbf{a} = [3 \;\; -2]$$

$$\mathbf{b} = [1 \;\; 5]$$

$$\mathbf{c} = [6 \;\; -3 \;\; 1]$$

$$\mathbf{d} = [2 \;\; -1 \;\; 3]$$

Find
(a) $\mathbf{a} + \mathbf{b}$
(b) $\mathbf{b} + \mathbf{a}$
(c) $\mathbf{b} - \mathbf{a}$
(d) $\mathbf{c} + \mathbf{d}$
(e) $\mathbf{c} - \mathbf{d}$
(f) The vector that is double the length of $\mathbf{a}$ and is in the same direction as $\mathbf{a}$.

(g) The vector that is double the length of **a** and is in the opposite direction to **a**.

(h) The vector that is double the length of **d** and is in the same direction as **d**.

(i) The magnitude of **a**

(j) The magnitude of **d**

(k) The dot product of **a** with **b**

(l) The dot product of **c** with **d**

(m) The transpose of **d**.

2 Given the following matrices

$$A = \begin{bmatrix} 1 & 2 \\ 4 & -5 \end{bmatrix} \qquad B = \begin{bmatrix} 1 & -4 & 0 \\ 2 & 1 & 2 \end{bmatrix}$$

Find

(a) a_{22}

(b) $A + A$

(c) The product AB

(d) The transpose of B

(e) The product AA^T

3 Repeat Exercise 2 for the following matrices

$$A = \begin{bmatrix} 4 & 6 & 3 \\ 2 & -3 & -2 \end{bmatrix} \qquad B = \begin{bmatrix} 1 & 1 & 3 \\ 3 & 2 & 5 \\ 2 & 2 & 1 \end{bmatrix}$$

4 Solve the equations

$$x_1 + 3x_2 = 8$$
$$2x_1 + 3x_2 = 10$$

5 Solve the equations

$$-2x_1 + 3x_2 = 11$$
$$4x_1 + x_2 = -1$$

6 Solve the equations

$$x_1 + 2x_2 + x_3 = 5$$
$$2x_1 + x_2 + 3x_3 = 9$$
$$x_1 + 2x_2 - x_3 = 1$$

7 Solve the equations

$$x_1 + x_2 + 2x_3 = 5$$
$$-x_1 + 3x_2 + 3x_3 = 14$$
$$3x_1 + x_2 - x_3 = -8$$

8 Solve the equations

$$x_1 + 2x_2 + x_3 = 0$$
$$2x_1 + x_2 + 3x_3 = 2$$
$$x_1 + 2x_2 - x_3 = 2$$

Determinants and applications of matrices

Introduction

In this chapter we continue with our study of matrices before concluding with some applications.

Determinants

Suppose that we have two equations:

$$a_{11}x_1 + a_{12}x_2 + b_1 = 0$$
$$a_{21}x_1 + a_{22}x_2 + b_2 = 0$$

it can be shown that a solution is given by

$$x_1 = (a_{12}b_2 - a_{22}b_1)/(a_{11}a_{22} - a_{12}a_{21})$$
$$x_2 = -(a_{11}b_2 - a_{21}b_1)/(a_{11}a_{22} - a_{12}a_{21})$$

provided that the denominator is nonzero. If we put the equations into the augmented matrix form we get

$$\begin{bmatrix} a_{11} & a_{12} & b_1 \\ a_{21} & a_{22} & b_2 \end{bmatrix}$$

From the augmented matrix, it is possible to construct three 2×2 matrices with the columns in their respective order: first column with the second column, first with the third and the second with the third.

$$\begin{bmatrix} a_{11} & a_{12} \\ a_{21} & a_{22} \end{bmatrix} \quad \begin{bmatrix} a_{11} & b_1 \\ a_{21} & b_2 \end{bmatrix} \quad \begin{bmatrix} a_{12} & b_1 \\ a_{22} & b_2 \end{bmatrix}$$

If you look back to the solution for x_1 and x_2 and compare the expressions in brackets with the above matrices you will see a relationship. The coefficients in brackets are all found by subtracting the product of the diagonal elements. For the first matrix we get

$$(a_{11}a_{22} - a_{21}a_{12})$$

which is the 'determinant' of the matrix $\begin{bmatrix} a_{11} & a_{12} \\ a_{21} & a_{22} \end{bmatrix}$. The determinant would usually be written:

$$\begin{vmatrix} a_{11} & a_{12} \\ a_{21} & a_{22} \end{vmatrix}$$

and in this example is a determinant of the second order.

Example 6.1

Find the three second-order determinants of the matrix

$$\begin{bmatrix} 1 & -2 & -3 \\ 1 & 1 & -6 \end{bmatrix}$$

Solution

We want the determinants of the three 2×2 matrices:

$$\begin{vmatrix} 1 & -2 \\ 1 & 1 \end{vmatrix} \quad \begin{vmatrix} 1 & -3 \\ 1 & -6 \end{vmatrix} \quad \begin{vmatrix} -2 & -3 \\ 1 & -6 \end{vmatrix}$$

The determinants are

$$(1 \times 1) - (1 \times -2) = 3$$
$$(1 \times -6) - (1 \times -3) = -3$$
$$(-2 \times -6) - (1 \times -3) = 15$$

There are higher-order determinants. For instance, a determinant of the third order is

$$\begin{vmatrix} a_{11} & a_{12} & a_{13} \\ a_{21} & a_{22} & a_{23} \\ a_{31} & a_{32} & a_{33} \end{vmatrix}$$

and has a value of

$$a_{11}a_{22}a_{33} - a_{11}a_{32}a_{23} + a_{12}a_{31}a_{23} - a_{12}a_{21}a_{33} + a_{13}a_{21}a_{32} - a_{13}a_{31}a_{22}$$

Minors and cofactors

The introduction of minors and cofactors leads to a systematic way of calculating higher-order determinants. Associated with each element of a third-order determinant is a second-order determinant. For element a_{ij}, the associated determinant M_{ij} is made up of the elements that are left after striking out row i and column j. The determinant M_{ij} is called the 'minor' of a_{ij}. For example, to find M_{21} we strike out row 2 and column 1:

$$\begin{vmatrix} a_{11} & a_{12} & a_{13} \\ a_{21} & a_{22} & a_{23} \\ a_{31} & a_{32} & a_{33} \end{vmatrix}$$

$$M_{21} = \begin{vmatrix} a_{12} & a_{13} \\ a_{32} & a_{33} \end{vmatrix}$$

We stated earlier, that for a matrix A its third-order determinant is

$$|A| = a_{11}a_{22}a_{33} - a_{11}a_{32}a_{23} + a_{12}a_{31}a_{23} - a_{12}a_{21}a_{33} + a_{13}a_{21}a_{32} - a_{13}a_{31}a_{22}$$

This can be rewritten as

$$|A| = a_{11}(a_{22}a_{33} - a_{32}a_{23}) - a_{12}(a_{21}a_{33} - a_{31}a_{23}) + a_{13}(a_{21}a_{32} - a_{31}a_{22})$$

$$|A| = a_{11}M_{11} - a_{12}M_{12} + a_{13}M_{13}$$

The determinant has been expressed using the minors for the elements in the top row of the third-order determinant. We could instead, use the minors for the other two rows or use the minors for a column. Therefore, for a third-order determinant we can calculate its value using minors in six different ways (because we have three rows and three columns). It is still not yet clear how we determine the sign for each product in $|A| = a_{11}M_{11} - a_{12}M_{12} + a_{13}M_{13}$. The sign is found from the array of signs. For example, for a third-order determinant the array of signs is

$$\begin{vmatrix} + & - & + \\ - & + & - \\ + & - & + \end{vmatrix}$$

So the first element of the first row is $+$ and the signs alternate between $+$ and $-$ as you work across a row or down a column. The sign array introduces the idea of the cofactor. For a matrix A with determinant $|A|$, the cofactor for element a_{ij} is written A_{ij} and is the signed minor of a_{ij}. For example,

$$A_{32} = -M_{32}$$

because the sign of a_{32} is $-$.

The determinant for

$$\begin{vmatrix} a_{11} & a_{12} & a_{13} \\ a_{21} & a_{22} & a_{23} \\ a_{31} & a_{32} & a_{33} \end{vmatrix}$$

can now be written as

$$a_{11}A_{11} + a_{12}A_{12} + a_{13}A_{13}$$

if the determinant is calculated using the first row.

Alternatively, if we use the first column the determinant is calculated from

$$a_{11}A_{11} + a_{21}A_{21} + a_{31}A_{31}$$

We could also use either of the other two rows or columns.

Example 6.2

Find the determinant of the matrix A.

$$A = \begin{bmatrix} 1 & 2 & 0 \\ 4 & 5 & 2 \\ 2 & 7 & 8 \end{bmatrix}$$

Solution
We shall use the first row

$$1 \times A_{11} + 2 \times A_{12} + 0 \times A_{13}$$

So we do not need to calculate the cofactor for the third entry in the first row since it is going to be multiplied by zero.

$$A_{11} = \begin{vmatrix} 5 & 2 \\ 7 & 8 \end{vmatrix} \quad A_{12} = -\begin{vmatrix} 4 & 2 \\ 2 & 8 \end{vmatrix}$$

$$A_{11} = 5 \times 8 - 7 \times 2 = 26$$
$$A_{12} = -(4 \times 8 - 2 \times 2) = -28$$

So the determinant is

$$|A| = 26 + 2 \times -28 = -30$$

Example 6.3

Find the determinant of the matrix A.

$$A = \begin{bmatrix} 2 & 5 & 3 & 1 \\ 5 & 3 & 0 & 8 \\ 8 & 0 & 0 & 4 \\ 9 & 2 & 1 & 0 \end{bmatrix}$$

Solution

For convenience we shall use the third row since it contains two zeros and therefore we shall not have to evaluate their cofactors.

$$|A| = 8 \times A_{31} + 4 \times A_{34}$$

$$A_{31} = \begin{vmatrix} 5 & 3 & 1 \\ 3 & 0 & 8 \\ 2 & 1 & 0 \end{vmatrix} \quad A_{34} = - \begin{vmatrix} 2 & 5 & 3 \\ 5 & 3 & 0 \\ 9 & 2 & 1 \end{vmatrix}$$

We now have to evaluate the two three-order determinants first.

$$|A_{31}| = 3 \times A_{21} + 8 \times A_{23} \quad \text{using the second row of } A_{31}$$

$$|A_{31}| = 3 \times - \begin{vmatrix} 3 & 1 \\ 1 & 0 \end{vmatrix} + 8 \times - \begin{vmatrix} 5 & 3 \\ 2 & 1 \end{vmatrix}$$

$$|A_{31}| = -3(0 - 1) - 8 \times (5 - 6)$$

$$= 11$$

$$|A_{34}| = -(5 \times A_{21} + 3 \times A_{22}) \quad \text{using the second row of } A_{34}$$

$$|A_{34}| = -\left(5 \times - \begin{vmatrix} 5 & 3 \\ 2 & 1 \end{vmatrix} + 3 \times \begin{vmatrix} 2 & 3 \\ 9 & 1 \end{vmatrix}\right)$$

$$|A_{34}| = -(5 \times -(5 - 6) + 3 \times (2 - 27))$$

$$= 70$$

So we now have

$$|A| = 8 \times 11 + 4 \times 70$$

$$= 368$$

Note that if you are still unsure of the sign that a cofactor takes it can be found quite easily by noting that the cofactor for element a_{ij} is

$$(-1)^{i+j}|A_{ij}|$$

So the sign that the determinant takes when working out the cofactor of a_{23} is

$$(-1)^{2+3} = -1$$

The technique we have employed to calculate the determinant in Example 6.3 relies on the repeated expansion of the cofactors; each cofactor is worked out from lower-order cofactors. This technique is not efficient for implementation on a computer. We shall introduce a different technique for calculating the determinant of a square matrix after presentation of the next example.

Example 6.4

Find the determinant of the matrix A.

$$A = \begin{bmatrix} 2 & 5 & 3 \\ 0 & 3 & 0 \\ 0 & 0 & 1 \end{bmatrix}$$

Solution

Note that all elements below the diagonal are zero; a matrix that has zeros below the diagonal is known as 'upper-triangular'. A matrix with zeros above the diagonal is known as 'lower-triangular' and both are examples of 'triangular matrices'. If we use the third row to calculate the determinant we have

$$|A| = 1 \times A_{33}$$

$$= \begin{vmatrix} 2 & 5 \\ 0 & 3 \end{vmatrix}$$

$$= 6$$

It can be shown that for a triangular matrix, its determinant is the product of its diagonal elements. So for the above example the determinant is simply

$$2 \times 3 \times 1 = 6$$

Finding a determinant by reduction to a triangular matrix

A square matrix that is in row-echelon form is triangular. This leads to an alternative technique for calculating the determinant of a matrix.

1. Reduce the matrix to row-echelon form using only row interchanges and row addition.

2. If in the process any row contains only zeros then the determinant is zero otherwise

$$|A| = (-1)^r \times (\text{Product of pivots})$$

where r is the number of row interchanges

Example 6.5

Find the determinant of the matrix A by transforming A to row-echelon form

$$A = \begin{bmatrix} 1 & 2 & 0 \\ 4 & 5 & 2 \\ 2 & 7 & 8 \end{bmatrix}$$

Solution

$$\begin{bmatrix} 1 & 2 & 0 \\ 4 & 5 & 2 \\ 2 & 7 & 8 \end{bmatrix}$$

$$\begin{bmatrix} 1 & 2 & 0 \\ 0 & -3 & 2 \\ 2 & 7 & 8 \end{bmatrix} \quad R_2 \rightarrow R_2 + -4R_1$$

$$\begin{bmatrix} 1 & 2 & 0 \\ 0 & -3 & 2 \\ 0 & 3 & 8 \end{bmatrix} \quad R_3 \rightarrow R_3 + -2R_1$$

$$\begin{bmatrix} 1 & 2 & 0 \\ 0 & -3 & 2 \\ 0 & 0 & 10 \end{bmatrix} \quad R_3 \rightarrow R_3 + R_2$$

There have been no row interchanges and the product of pivots is the product of diagonal elements and so

$$|A| = 1 \times -3 \times 10 = -30$$

Example 6.6

Find the determinant of the matrix A by reducing to row-echelon form

$$A = \begin{bmatrix} 2 & 1 & 5 \\ 2 & 1 & 8 \\ 4 & 5 & 2 \end{bmatrix}$$

Solution

$$\begin{bmatrix} 2 & 1 & 5 \\ 0 & 0 & 3 \\ 0 & 3 & -8 \end{bmatrix} \quad \begin{matrix} R_2 \rightarrow R_2 - R_1 \\ R_3 \rightarrow R_3 - 2R_1 \end{matrix}$$

$$\begin{bmatrix} 2 & 1 & 3 \\ 0 & 3 & -8 \\ 0 & 0 & 3 \end{bmatrix} \quad \text{interchange rows 2 and 3}$$

There has been one row interchange and so the determinant is

$$|A| = (-1)^1 \times 2 \times 3 \times 3$$
$$= -18$$

> **Properties of determinants**
> 1. If every element of a row of a determinant is zero then the value of the determinant is zero.
> 2. If two rows of a square matrix are equal, then the value of the determinant is zero.
> 3. For any square matrix, the value of its determinant is equal to the value of the determinant of the transposed matrix.
> 4. If any single row of a square matrix is multiplied by a scalar k, then the value of the determinant is multiplied by k.
> 5. If two different rows of a square matrix are interchanged, the determinant of the matrix becomes $-|A|$.
> 6. The sum of products of a row of a square matrix with the cofactors of another row is zero.

> The 'adjoint' of a matrix is obtained by replacing the elements of the transposed matrix with their cofactors.

Example 6.7

Find the adjoint matrix of A, written *adj A*.

$$A = \begin{bmatrix} 2 & 1 & 5 \\ 2 & 1 & 8 \\ 4 & 5 & 2 \end{bmatrix}$$

Solution

The transpose of A is

$$A^T = \begin{bmatrix} 2 & 2 & 4 \\ 1 & 1 & 5 \\ 5 & 8 & 2 \end{bmatrix}$$

Taking the cofactors of A^T we get:

$$adj\ A = \begin{bmatrix} -38 & 23 & 3 \\ 28 & -16 & -6 \\ 6 & -6 & 0 \end{bmatrix}$$

By using Property 6 it can be shown that

$$A\,adjA = |A|\,I$$

where I is the identity matrix. This leads to a way of finding the 'inverse' of a square matrix. The inverse of a matrix A, written A^{-1}, has the following relationship with the identity matrix

$$AA^{-1} = I$$

So a matrix multiplied by its inverse gives the identity matrix. From $A\,adjA = |A|\,I$, we get

$$A^{-1} = \frac{1}{|A|}\,adjA$$

Example 6.8

Find the inverse of the matrix

$$A = \begin{bmatrix} 2 & 1 & 5 \\ 2 & 1 & 8 \\ 4 & 5 & 2 \end{bmatrix}$$

Solution

From Example 6.6 we know that $|A| = -18$ and from Example 6.7 we have

$$adj\,A = \begin{bmatrix} -38 & 23 & 3 \\ 28 & -16 & -6 \\ 6 & -6 & 0 \end{bmatrix}$$

and so

$$A^{-1} = -\frac{1}{18} \begin{bmatrix} -38 & 23 & 3 \\ 28 & -16 & -6 \\ 6 & -6 & 0 \end{bmatrix}$$

We can check the result by noting that

$$\begin{bmatrix} 2 & 1 & 5 \\ 2 & 1 & 8 \\ 4 & 5 & 2 \end{bmatrix} \begin{bmatrix} \dfrac{38}{18} & -\dfrac{23}{18} & -\dfrac{3}{18} \\ -\dfrac{28}{18} & \dfrac{16}{18} & \dfrac{6}{18} \\ -\dfrac{6}{18} & \dfrac{6}{18} & 0 \end{bmatrix} = \begin{bmatrix} 1 & 0 & 0 \\ 0 & 1 & 0 \\ 0 & 0 & 1 \end{bmatrix}$$

In Chapter 4 we learnt what an inverse function is. Often a matrix will be used to map a vector. For example you might wish to centre and rotate an image to a constant position for the purpose of object recognition. You can undo the rotation by performing the inverse mapping using the inverse matrix.

6.1

Answers appear in Appendix A.

1 Calculate $\begin{vmatrix} 2 & -2 \\ 1 & 3 \end{vmatrix}$ and $\begin{vmatrix} 1 & 2 \\ 3 & 1 \end{vmatrix}$

2 Give the minors for the second column of A then use the minors to calculate the determinant for A

$$A = \begin{bmatrix} 2 & 4 & 1 \\ 2 & 0 & -1 \\ 1 & 0 & 2 \end{bmatrix}$$

3 Find the inverse for A in Question 2.

Summary

- The determinant of the matrix $\begin{bmatrix} a_{11} & a_{12} \\ a_{21} & a_{22} \end{bmatrix}$ is written as

$$\begin{vmatrix} a_{11} & a_{12} \\ a_{21} & a_{22} \end{vmatrix}$$

and its value is $(a_{11}a_{22} - a_{21}a_{12})$. This is called a second-order determinant. A determinant of the third order is

$$\begin{vmatrix} a_{11} & a_{12} & a_{13} \\ a_{21} & a_{22} & a_{23} \\ a_{31} & a_{32} & a_{33} \end{vmatrix}$$

and has a value of

$$a_{11}a_{22}a_{33} - a_{11}a_{32}a_{23} + a_{12}a_{31}a_{23} - a_{12}a_{21}a_{33} + a_{13}a_{21}a_{32} - a_{13}a_{31}a_{22}$$

- For matrix A, the above can be written as

$$|A| = a_{11}(a_{22}a_{33} - a_{32}a_{23}) - a_{12}(a_{21}a_{33} - a_{31}a_{23}) + a_{13}(a_{21}a_{32} - a_{31}a_{22})$$

$$|A| = a_{11}M_{11} - a_{12}M_{12} + a_{13}M_{13}$$

- Associated with each element of a third-order determinant is a second-order determinant. For element a_{ij}, the associated determinant M_{ij} is made up of the elements that are left after striking out row i and column j. The determinant M_{ij} is called the minor of a_{ij}. For example, to find M_{21} we strike out row 2 and column 1:

$$\begin{vmatrix} a_{11} & a_{12} & a_{13} \\ a_{21} & a_{22} & a_{23} \\ a_{31} & a_{32} & a_{33} \end{vmatrix}$$

$$M_{21} = \begin{vmatrix} a_{12} & a_{13} \\ a_{32} & a_{33} \end{vmatrix}$$

the cofactor for element a_{ij} is

$$(-1)^{i+j}|A_{ij}|$$

- A determinant can be found by reduction to a triangular matrix.
- The adjoint of a matrix is obtained by replacing the elements of the transposed matrix with their cofactors.
  The inverse of a matrix A can be found from

$$A^{-1} = \frac{1}{|A|} \, adj \, A$$

where $adjA$ is the adjoint of A.

Applications of vectors and matrices

There are many applications of vectors and matrices within science and engineering. For computer practitioners a major application is the efficient representation of information and the development of what are known as 'compiled techniques' for efficient calculations.

Navigation

The aircraft pilots and sailors of today can take advantage of computerised navigation equipment. Although they do not have to know how these computer systems are implemented they do need to appreciate the concept of vectors so that they can identify any unsuitable instructions issued by the computer because of the incorrect input of information, and in some types of non-airline flying there can be a need to resort to traditional methods when equipment fails. Suppose we are flying an aircraft on a heading of 050 degrees with an airspeed of 120 kt and the wind is blowing from 140 degrees at 30 kt. We need to find our actual heading and groundspeed. Well, we can get an idea of our heading and speed by plotting the aircraft's velocity vector and the wind vector (see Figure 6.1). From the diagram of

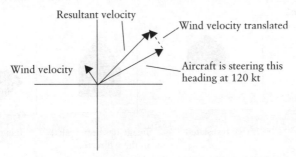

Figure 6.1 The plotting of an aircraft's velocity vector and wind vector to resolve the actual heading and the speed over the ground.

velocities we can see that the aircraft's actual track (resultant direction of travel) will be less than 050 degrees and its ground speed will be slightly greater than 120 kt. We could use trigonometry to calculate the resultant vector. Pilots are trained to use a mechanical flight computer on which they plot the vectors; this is a good exercise even though they will probably use computers during their careers.

Image processing

In image processing, matrices are used for the representation of images, the compression of images and other general forms of image processing.

Suppose that we have a polygon-shaped image in the x-y plane as shown in Figure 6.2. Each pixel (a point inside the shape) is represented by a row vector giving its coordinates – (every point is a black pixel. All the pixels together form a matrix and this matrix can be multiplied by transformation matrices to perform translation, scaling and rotation. For example, the transformation matrix to rotate the image through an angle θ is

$$\begin{bmatrix} \cos\theta & -\sin\theta \\ \sin\theta & \cos\theta \end{bmatrix}$$

Another form of transformation that is used to preprocess an image for object recognition is the Hotelling transform. One of the difficulties with identifying an object is that the object might appear at different positions in the image and at different orientations on different occasions. The recognition of an object can be greatly assisted if the variation in an object's position and rotation is removed or at least reduced as much as is possible. The aircraft in Figure 6.3 can be rotated and shifted to a fixed point of reference. The image is rotated by finding what are called the 'eigenvectors' of the image. The eigenvectors are computed using methods that build on those introduced in this chapter. A matrix of the eigenvectors provides a transformation matrix and the product of the image matrix with this transformation matrix gives the desired rotation.

The Hotelling transform is more commonly known as Principal Component Analysis (PCA) in the field of statistics. PCA is a very useful technique for finding trends in large data sets and for removing redundant information. The computing of eigenvectors is such a fundamental requirement for many engineering and scientific applications that it is provided as a standard tool in most mathematical and statistical software packages.

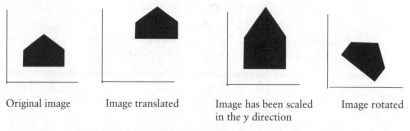

Original image   Image translated   Image has been scaled   Image rotated
                                              in the y direction

Figure 6.2   The transformation of images can be achieved by multiplying a matrix
              representation of the image with transformation matrices.

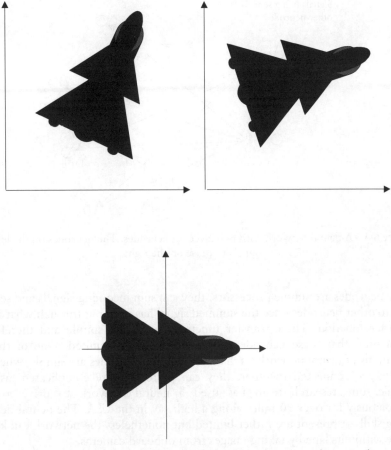

Figure 6.3 The aircraft can be rotated to a fixed point of reference as shown in the image at the bottom.

Implementing neural networks

A topic that is now taught to many (if not most) engineering and computing students is neural computing. It also appears on the syllabus of many psychology degrees. Neural networks are an exciting development and these computing machines have attracted more attention over the last ten to fifteen years. Their application ranges from the diagnosis of the state of health (i.e., mechanical condition) of a helicopter to predicting the price of shares on the stock markets. A neural network is basically a collection of simple processors known as neurodes that communicate with each other along weighted connections. By communication we mean that a neurode can send a signal (typically a real value) to other neurodes. The connection along which the signal travels serves either to excite (amplify) or inhibit (reduce the effect of) a signal. This excitation or inhibition is achieved by multiplying the signal by the connection's weighted value. A network is illustrated in Figure 6.4.

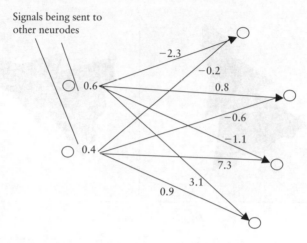

Figure 6.4 A neural network with two layers of neurodes. The neurodes on the left send signals to those on the right.

The neurodes are simple processors; they can sum incoming signals and send on a signal to other neurodes once the summed signal has been put through what is called a transfer function. These transfer functions really are simple and therefore the computation that these neurodes can perform is very limited. One of the great fascinations of neural networks is that although the neurodes are simple, when many of them are connected together, they can perform quite complicated tasks. For example, one research team has used a neural network to drive a vehicle autonomously for over 90 miles along a highway in the USA. The neural network's driving skills at present are rather limited but nonetheless the network can keep the vehicle within its lane by taking images from onboard cameras.

Neural networks are not programmed in a conventional sense – instead, they learn to perform a task. For example, the autonomous vehicle learns by observing human drivers.

Neural networks are designed to be implemented in parallel hardware but most of the research and development work is done using software simulations. It is typical to represent a neural network using matrices. For example, the matrix of connections in Figure 6.4 would be written as:

$$\begin{bmatrix} -2.3 & 0.8 & -1.1 & 3.1 \\ -0.2 & -0.6 & 7.3 & 0.9 \end{bmatrix}$$

where a row indexes one of the two neurodes on the left and the columns index those neurodes on the right. If the signals being sent out by the two neurodes on the left are represented by a row vector, the summed inputs to those neurodes on the right can be calculated from a simple matrix multiplication:

$$[0.6 \quad 0.4] \begin{bmatrix} -2.3 & 0.8 & -1.1 & 3.1 \\ -0.2 & -0.6 & 7.3 & 0.9 \end{bmatrix} = [-1.5 \quad 0.2 \quad 2.3 \quad 2.2]$$

EXERCISES

Answers appear in Appendix B.

1 Calculate $\begin{vmatrix} 2 & -2 \\ 1 & 3 \end{vmatrix}$ and $\begin{vmatrix} 1 & 2 \\ 3 & 1 \end{vmatrix}$

2 Give the minors for the first column of A then use the minors to calculate the determinant for A

$$A = \begin{bmatrix} 1 & 4 & 1 \\ 2 & -3 & -1 \\ 1 & 0 & 3 \end{bmatrix}$$

3 Evaluate:

(a) $\begin{vmatrix} 3 & 1 & 2 \\ 2 & -2 & 4 \\ -3 & 7 & 3 \end{vmatrix}$

(b) $\begin{vmatrix} 2 & 1 & 5 \\ 2 & -2 & 6 \\ 3 & 9 & 3 \end{vmatrix}$

(c) $\begin{vmatrix} 1 & 1 & 9 \\ 1 & 0 & 4 \\ 5 & 0 & 2 \end{vmatrix}$

(d) $\begin{vmatrix} 1 & 1 & 7 \\ 1 & 0 & 4 \\ 0 & 0 & -2 \end{vmatrix}$

4 Given that the determinant of a square matrix is −20, what will be the value of a determinant that is the same matrix but with a single row that is a multiple of 3 of the original matrix?

5 Given that the determinant of the matrix

$$\begin{bmatrix} 4 & 4 & 3 \\ 2 & 5 & 1 \\ 1 & -2 & 5 \end{bmatrix}$$

is 45 , without performing any calculation what is the determinant of the matrix

$$\begin{bmatrix} 2 & 5 & 1 \\ 4 & 4 & 3 \\ 1 & -2 & 5 \end{bmatrix}$$

6 Find the inverse of the matrix

$$\begin{bmatrix} 2 & 6 \\ 1 & 8 \end{bmatrix}$$

7 Find the inverse of the matrix

$$\begin{bmatrix} 2 & 5 & 1 \\ 4 & 4 & 3 \\ 1 & -2 & 5 \end{bmatrix}$$

7

Graphs

Introduction

There are numerous examples of graphs. The map of the London underground that passengers use on a daily basis to work out connecting trains to get to their destination is an example of a graph. An organisation chart of a company is another example and so too is a flow chart that a programmer might draw to express the implementation of an algorithm. The way in which the graph is drawn depends on the information that it is designed to represent. For instance, the London underground is an abstraction of the real tube lines that connect stations; the map does not show all the twists and bends in the track as this would clutter the map and is of no benefit to the passengers. Also, instead of showing the distance between stations it would be more appropriate to indicate average travel times between stations. On the other hand, a map used by a car driver will show distances between locations. Graphs have numerous applications and a number of algorithms have been built over the years for finding the shortest path between two points or for scanning graphs in search of information, etc.

This chapter begins with an introduction to graph terminology followed by the matrix representation of a graph for implementation on the computer. A couple of useful algorithms are introduced. The chapter then looks at trees and tree traversal algorithms. Finally, some applications are studied; an efficient way of storing and searching for words, a simple text compression technique, and an indication of the significant role that graph theory plays for developing artificial intelligence systems which are programs that are designed to perform tasks that humans are good at like medical diagnosis, robot planning, language understanding, etc.

Definition of a graph

This section will give a more formal definition of a graph and will introduce some general terms.

The word graph is used in a rather loose way to denote a number of visual forms of presentation of information. For example, bar charts and pie charts (see Figure 7.1) are sometimes referred to as graphs and we often talk about 'graphical user interface' but in this chapter our use of the word graph has a strict mathematical meaning.

A graph is made up of three components:
- A non-empty set of 'vertices' or 'nodes'
- A set of 'edges' or 'arcs'
- A function that associates each edge with an unordered pair of vertices

According to this definition of a graph, the map of the London underground is a graph and so is the neural network we sketched at the end of Chapter 6 but the bar chart and pie chart are not examples.

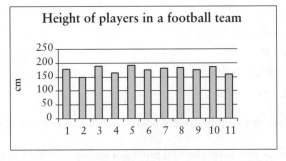

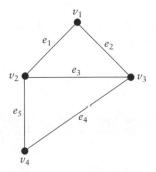

Figure 7.1 Example of bar chart (top) and pie chart (bottom).

Example 7.1

For the graph in Figure 7.2, list the set of vertices, the set of edges and the functions that associates each edge with an unordered pair of vertices.

Figure 7.2

Solution

The set of vertices is

$$\{v_1, v_2, v_3, v_4\}$$

the set of edges

$$\{e_1, e_2, e_3, e_4, e_5\}$$

and functions

$$f(e_1) = v_1 - v_2$$
$$f(e_2) = v_1 - v_3$$
$$f(e_3) = v_2 - v_3$$
$$f(e_4) = v_3 - v_4$$
$$f(e_5) = v_2 - v_4$$

Note that the functions simply relate each edge to the vertices at each end (i.e., the endpoints).

The two vertices that form the end points of an edge are said to be 'adjacent'. So in Figure 7.2 v_1 and v_2 are adjacent and v_1 and v_3 are adjacent, etc. An edge that has both endpoints as the same vertex is a 'loop'. For example, e_4 in Figure 7.3 is a loop. Two edges with the same endpoints are 'parallel edges'. For example, e_1 and e_5 are parallel edges. A simple graph has no loops or parallel edges. The 'degree' of a vertex is the number of edge ends that meet at that vertex. For example, all the edges in Figure 7.3 have degree 3 apart from v_3. Note that a loop adds degree 2 to the vertex.

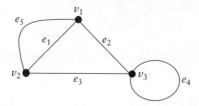

Figure 7.3   A graph showing a loop, and parallel edges.

Example 7.2

For each of the graphs in Figure 7.4 note down the degree of each vertex and state whether the graph is simple or not.

Solution

(a) The degree of each vertex is

$$v_1 = 3$$
$$v_2 = 2$$
$$v_3 = 3$$

The graph is not a simple graph.

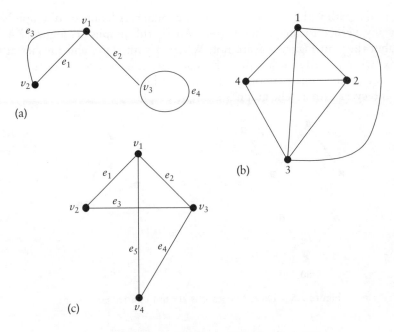

(a)

(b)

(c)

Figure 7.4 Graphs used for Example 7.2.

(b) The degree of each vertex is

> vertex 1 = 4
> vertex 2 = 3
> vertex 3 = 4
> vertex 4 = 3

The graph is not a simple graph because there are parallel edges connecting vertices 1 and 3.

(c) The degree of each vertex is

> $v_1 = 3$
> $v_2 = 2$
> $v_3 = 3$
> $v_4 = 2$

The graph is a simple graph.

> A path from a starting vertex v_1 to a finish vertex v_k is a sequence of vertices and edges:
>
> $$v_1, e_1, v_2, e_2, \ldots, v_{k-1}, e_{k-1}, v_k$$

The 'length' of a path is the number of edges it contains. A 'connected' graph has a path from any vertex to any other vertex. All of the graphs in Figure 7.4 are connected but those in Figure 7.5 are not. Where a path starts and finishes at the same vertex, with no vertex other than the start vertex occurring more than once, and no edge occurring more than once, the path is called a 'cycle'. An 'acyclic' graph is one with no cycles. An acyclic graph is a simple graph.

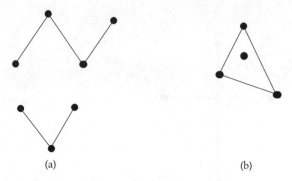

(a)   (b)

Figure 7.5   These two graphs are not connected.

Example 7.3

For the graph in Figure 7.6, sketch a cycle of length 3 and one of length 4.

Figure 7.6   Graph used in Example 7.3.

Solution
Note that any of the vertices shown on the paths could be the starting point and the path could be reversed in each case.

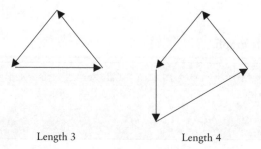

Length 3   Length 4

Often we will want to show that an edge is to be traversed in one direction only. For instance, signals in a circuit might be designed to travel in one direction. A graph that specifies a direction for each edge is called a 'directed' graph and is defined by

- A non-empty set of vertices or nodes
- A set of edges or arcs
- A function that associates each edge with an ordered pair of vertices.

Figure 7.7 is an example of a directed graph. Notice that vertex 3 cannot be reached from any other vertex whereas from 3 you can traverse to any other vertex. Also there are two paths from 3 to 2; the first is direct from 3 to 2 and the second from 3 to 1 then from 1 to 2.

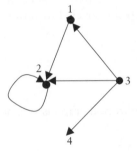

Figure 7.7   An example of a directed graph.

Labelled and weighted graphs

A labelled graph has the vertices labelled. An example is the London underground map where each tube station is given a name. A weighted graph associates each edge with a numerical value (often simply called 'weight'). A road map where edges are marked with distances is an example of a weighted graph and another example is the neural network sketched in Chapter 6.

The computer representation of a graph

Sometimes graphs are represented using a linked list where a list of vertices is stored with each vertex storing a reference to an adjacent vertex. A convenient form of storage and the one that we shall concentrate on is called an 'adjacency matrix'.

An adjacency matrix for a graph with n vertices is an $n \times n$ matrix where the element at row i and column j gives the number of edges connecting vertex i to vertex j.

Example 7.4

Give the adjacency matrix for the graph in Figure 7.8

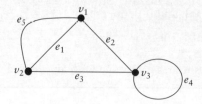

Figure 7.8   Graph used for Example 7.4.

Solution

Entry (1, 1) is 0 because vertex 1 does not connect to itself, unlike vertex 3 (entry (3, 3)). Entry (1, 2) is 2 because there are two edges connecting vertex 1 to vertex 2 and likewise for entry (2, 1) going from vertex 2 to vertex 1.

$$\begin{bmatrix} 0 & 2 & 1 \\ 2 & 0 & 1 \\ 1 & 1 & 1 \end{bmatrix}$$

The adjacency matrix of an undirected graph is symmetric.

Example 7.5

Give the adjacency matrix for the directed graph in Figure 7.9.

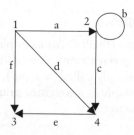

Figure 7.9   Graph used for Examples 7.5 and 7.6.

Solution

$$\begin{bmatrix} 0 & 1 & 1 & 1 \\ 0 & 1 & 0 & 1 \\ 0 & 0 & 0 & 0 \\ 0 & 0 & 1 & 0 \end{bmatrix}$$

The adjacency matrix contains a lot of information. The number of vertices corresponds to the number of rows (and number of columns), the sum of all entries gives the number of edges in the graph, a matrix with only 0 and 1 for entries has no parallel edges and any loop will show up as a non-zero entry on the main diagonal (entries at i, j where $i = j$).

The matrix representation of a graph is useful for computing how many paths there are of a certain length between two vertices. Paths are an important concept. For example, a telephone network must be constructed to allow any two subscribers to communicate. It is highly unlikely that both subscribers will have a direct connection (i.e., are endpoints of an edge) but there should be a connection available by traversing several edges. If we have an adjacency matrix A, then the product AA (matrix multiplication) gives the number of paths of length 2 between any two vertices. To see this we shall look at an example.

Example 7.6

For the graph in Figure 7.9, consider that the graph is not directed (imagine no arrows).

1. List all the paths of length 1, length 2, length 3 from vertex 1 to 2.

2. Give the adjacency matrix, A

3. Give AA and AAA

Solution

1. Paths of length 1 from vertex 1 to 2 is simply a.

   Paths of length 2 from vertex 1 to 2 are ab, dc.

   Paths of length 3 from vertex 1 to 2 are 1a2a1a2, 1a2c4c2, 1a2b2b2, 1d4d1a2, 1d4c2b2, 1f3f1a2, 1f3e4c2

2.
$$A = \begin{bmatrix} 0 & 1 & 1 & 1 \\ 1 & 1 & 0 & 1 \\ 1 & 0 & 0 & 1 \\ 1 & 1 & 1 & 0 \end{bmatrix}$$

3.
$$AA = \begin{bmatrix} 3 & 2 & 1 & 2 \\ 2 & 3 & 2 & 2 \\ 1 & 2 & 2 & 1 \\ 2 & 2 & 1 & 3 \end{bmatrix}$$

$$AAA = \begin{bmatrix} 5 & 7 & 5 & 6 \\ 7 & 7 & 4 & 7 \\ 5 & 4 & 2 & 5 \\ 6 & 7 & 5 & 5 \end{bmatrix}$$

Notice that the entry (1, 2) in A gives the number of paths of length 1 from vertex 1 to 2, AA the number of paths of length 2 and AAA the number of paths of length 3. It is more usual to write A^2 instead of AA and A^3 instead of AAA and n products as A^n. So to find the number of paths of length n between any two vertices we compute A^n.

7.1

Answers appear in Appendix A.

1 For the graph in Figure 7.10
  (a) Is the graph connected?
  (b) List the degree of each vertex
  (c) Give the graph's adjacency matrix
  (d) Sketch a cycle of length 4
  (e) The number of paths of length 2 between all vertices

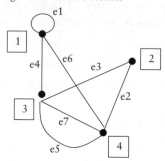

Figure 7.10

Euler path

One task that many of us have done as a child is to sketch the edges of the envelope in Figure 7.11 without taking our pencil off the paper and without going over the same edge twice. See which vertices allow you to follow the arrows to every vertex without covering the same edge twice. The type of path outlined in the above problem is known as an 'Euler' (pronounced 'oiler') path after the Swiss mathematician Leonhard Euler who in 1736 solved the Königsberg bridge problem. The city of Königsberg has a river that flows around an island and has several bridges as shown in Figure 7.12. The problem was to see if a person could walk through the city crossing each bridge only once. Euler's solution was to represent the problem as a graph where the bridges are edges and the land-masses are vertices.

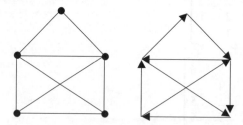

Figure 7.11   This graph has several Euler paths.

> A graph G has an Euler path if it has either two vertices of odd degree or no vertices of odd degree.

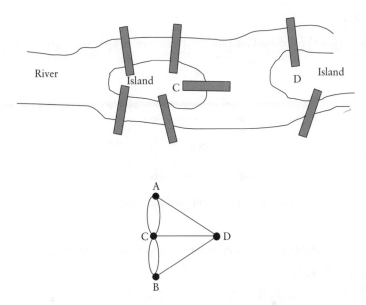

Figure 7.12 The Königsberg bridge problem.

The Königsberg graph has all vertices of odd degree and so no Euler path exists. Our envelope on the other hand has two vertices of odd degree.

Euler's theorem allows us to tell if an Euler path exists but we still need an algorithm for finding such paths. To find an Euler path we can use 'Fleury's algorithm'.

Fleury's algorithm

To create a list V of all vertices and a list E of all edges, keep a list VS of all vertices visited in sequence and a list of edges ES traversed in sequence. VS and ES start empty.

1. Start at a vertex with an odd degree if one exists, otherwise start at any vertex. Call the vertex v and add v to VS.
2. Stop if there are no edges remaining at v.
3. If v has exactly one edge remaining
    denote the edge as e and remove e from E and v from V. Call the other endpoint of e, w
   else
    choose an edge whose removal still keeps the remaining graph connected. Call the edge e and the other endpoint w. Remove e from E.
4. Add w to the end of VS and e to the end of ES, replace v by w and go to step 2.

Example 7.7

Use Fleury's algorithm to find an Euler path for the graph in Figure 7.13.

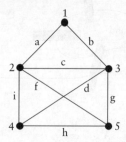

Figure 7.13   Graph used for Example 7.7.

Solution
Note that there is deliberately no edge labelled as e. So we have:

$V = [1, 2, 3, 4, 5]$
$E = [a, b, c, d, f, g, h, i]$
$VS = [\,]$
$ES = [\,]$

Step 1
Vertex 4 has odd degree and so $v = 4$. $VS = [4]$

Step 2
There are edges at v and so continue.

Step 3
There is more than one edge. We can remove any edge connected to v and still keep the graph connected. We shall choose i. So $e = i$ and $w = 2$ (the other endpoint of i).

Step 4

$VS = [4, 2]$ ES [i]
$v = 2$

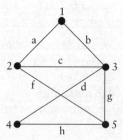

Step 2
There are edges at vertex 2.

Step 3
Remove edge a; the graph still remains connected.

$e = $ a. $w = 1$.

Step 4

> $VS = [4, 2, 1]$ *ES* [i, a]
>
> $v = 1$

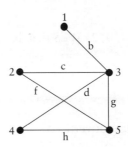

Step 2
One edge remaining at vertex 1

Step 3

> $w = 3$. $e = $ b.

Step 4

> $VS = [4, 2, 1, 3]$ *ES* [i, a, b]
>
> $v = 3$

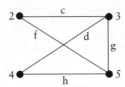

Step 2
Edges remaining at 3.

Step 3
Have more than one edge at 3. Removal of any will keep the graph connected. We shall remove edge c.

> $e = $ c. $w = 2$.

Step 4

> $VS = [4, 2, 1, 3, 2]$ *ES* [i, a, b, c]
>
> $v = 2$

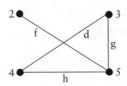

Step 2
There is an edge remaining at vertex 2.

Step 3
There is only one edge remaining, f, and so f is removed.

> $e = $ f. $w = 5$.

Step 4

$VS = [4, 2, 1, 3, 2, 5]$ ES [i, a, b, c, f]
$v = 5$

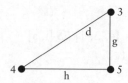

Step 2
There are two edges at vertex 5.

Step 3
We can remove either h or g and the graph remains connected. We shall choose g.

$e = g, w = 3$.

Step 4

$VS = [4, 2, 1, 3, 2, 5, 3]$ ES [i, a, b, c, f, g]
$v = 3$

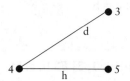

Step 2
There is one edge at vertex 3.

Step 3.
We remove d

$e = d, w = 4$

Step 4

$VS = [4, 2, 1, 3, 2, 5, 3, 4]$ ES [i, a, b, c, f, g, d]
$v = 4$

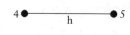

Step 2
One edge remaining at 4.

Step 3.

$e = h, w = 5$

Step 4

$VS = [4, 2, 1, 3, 2, 5, 3, 4, 5]$ ES [i, a, b, c, f, g, d, h]
$v = 5$

Step 2
No edges left so we stop.

The list *ES* gives the order of traversal to sketch out the Euler path.

We did not bother maintaining the lists *E* and *V* because it is easier to work with a sketch when using pencil and paper. We made a number of arbitrary choices between which edge to remove at several stages. You could repeat the procedure and choose to remove other edges with the result of alternative paths.

An Euler path visits every edge exactly once. A 'Hamiltonian' path, on the other hand, visits every vertex exactly once.

7.2

Answer appears in Appendix A.

1 Use Fleury's algorithm to find an Euler path for Figure 7.10

Trees

A tree is a connected acyclic (no cycles) graph. It is more common with trees to use the term node instead of vertex. A tree is drawn with a single root node from which branches lead to other nodes and in turn branches reach out from these nodes. An example tree is given in Figure 7.14.

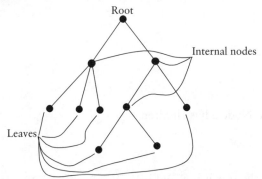

Figure 7.14   Example of a tree.

Each node has either one or more branches hanging from it or no branches. A branch is terminated with another node. A node with no hanging branches is a 'leaf' or 'terminal' node. A node with hanging branches is an 'internal' or 'nonterminal' node. Nodes that are connected via branches have an association. One node in the association is the parent node and the other the child node. For example, in Figure 7.15, node a is the parent of nodes (b, c) and (b, c) are the children of a. Similarly (d, e, f) are the children of b and b is the parent of (d, e, f).

A tree is known as a 'recursive' structure since any tree with more than one node can be seen as made up of other trees. For example, in Figure 7.15, node b can be seen as the root of a tree (a subtree of the whole tree) and c can be seen as the root of another and so too for g. By observing this recursive structure we can represent a tree as a list of leaf nodes. We generate the list from the bottom up. We shall use Figure 7.15 as an example.

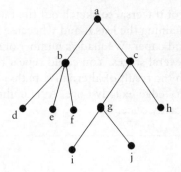

Figure 7.15   Tree with labelled nodes.

To build the list we shall start from the internal node that is furthest from the root node a. We start at g and write the children of g in parentheses:

(i, j)

Working up the tree from g to its parent we have c. Node c has children g and h:

(g, h)

we replace g with its children

((i, j), h)

The parent of c is a. Node a has children

(b, c)

and replacing c (by the tree it is a root of)

(b, ((i, j), h))

Finally we can replace b with its children

(d, e, f)

to get

((d, e, f), ((i, j), h))

Note that the list representation presented here only keeps explicit labels for leaf nodes.

The 'depth' of a node is the length of the path from the root node to the node and the 'height' of a tree is the maximum depth of any node.

Example 7.8

Answer the following for the tree in Figure 7.16

1. Which node is the root node?
2. Which nodes are the children of c?
3. Which node is the parent node of nodes f and g?
4. What is the depth of node d?
5. What is the height of the tree?
6. Write down the tree in list notation that has node c as its root.

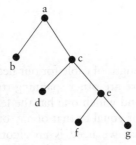

Figure 7.16 Tree used in Example 7.8.

Solution
1. a;   2. d, e;   3. e;   4. 2;   5. 3;   6. (d (f, g)).

Minimum spanning tree

Suppose you need to network a number of computers and each computer is located in a different office over a rather large site. The different localities can be represented using a weighted graph like the one shown in Figure 7.17. The weights (the numbers on the edges) represent the distance in metres between each office. The figure shows each office connected to every other office. So the graph shows all possible connections. The graphs in Figure 7.18 are all subgraphs of the graph in Figure 7.17. A subgraph H of a graph G contains a subset of the edges and vertices of G and each edge in H will have the same endpoints as in G. The subgraphs in Figure 7.18 are not any old subgraph: each subgraph has all of the vertices of the graph in Figure 7.17. When a subgraph H of a graph G contains all of the vertices found in G and remains connected, the subgraph is known as a 'spanning tree'. So all of the graphs in Figure 7.18 are spanning trees. Note that a spanning tree must have no cycles otherwise it is not a tree.

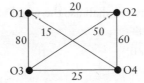

Figure 7.17 A weighted graph of office locations.

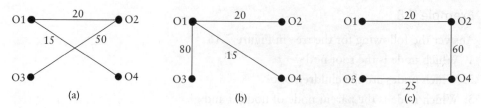

Figure 7.18 Selection of subgraphs from the graph in Figure 7.17.

If we add the weights on the paths in each figure we get the total weights:

(a) $20 + 15 + 50 = 85$

(b) $80 + 20 + 15 = 115$

(c) $60 + 20 + 25 = 105$

So if we wished to reduce the length of cable for our network it would be best to use the tree in Figure 7.18(a). There are other spanning trees for our network that we have not drawn. How do we find which one has the least total weight? A spanning tree whose weight is less than or equal to that of any other spanning tree is called a 'minimum spanning tree'. What we need is an algorithm to find this minimum spanning tree and for that we can use Kruskal's algorithm. The algorithm is fairly simple.

> **Kruskal's algorithm**
>
> Place all of the edges of the graph in a list W in the order of increasing weight.
> Use another list E to store the edges that make up the spanning tree.
> E starts as an empty list.
> $i = 0$
> while i is less than the number of edges in G
>
>   if the edge e_i associated with weight w_i plus the edges currently in E form an acyclic graph add e_i to E
> $i = i + 1$

Example 7.9

Use Kruskal's algorithm to find the minimum spanning tree for the graph in Figure 7.17.

Solution

Since all the weights are different we shall use the weights to denote the edges to save us generating labels for each edge.

   $W = [15, 20, 25, 50, 60, 80]$

   $i = 0$

   $E = [\,]$

$w_0 = 15$. There are no edges in E and so we add 15 to E.

$$E = [15]$$

$w_1 = 20$. The edge with weight 20 and weight 15 together is still acyclic so

$$E = [15, 20]$$

$w_2 = 25$. The edge with weight 25, 20 and weight 15 togther is still acyclic so

$$E = [15, 20, 25]$$

$w_3 = 50$. The edge with weight 50 plus those in E would create a cycle so 50 is not added

$$E = [15, 20, 25]$$

$w_6 = 60$. The edge with weight 60 plus those in E would create a cycle so 80 is not added

$$E = [15, 20, 25]$$

$w_5 = 80$. The edge with weight 80 plus those in E would create a cycle so 80 is not added

$$E = [15, 20, 25]$$

The loop ends and the list E defines the minimum spanning tree.

Example 7.10

Use Kruskal's algorithm to find the minimum spanning tree for the graph in Figure 7.19.

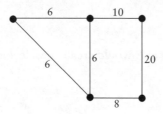

Figure 7.19   Graph used for Example 7.10.

Solution
First we shall label the edges using letters of the alphabet because we have more than one edge with the same weight and so we cannot use a weight as a unique identifier for an edge. The graph with edge labels is shown in Figure 7.20. Notice that for

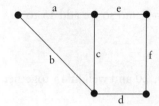

Figure 7.20   Graph in Figure 7.19 with edge labels.

convenience, the edges have been labelled in alphabetical order according to increasing weight; we could have labelled any of the edges with a weight value of 6 as a.

$i = 0$

$W = [a, b, c, d, e, f]$

$E = [ ]$

$w_0 = a$. There are no edges in E and so we add a to E.

$E = [a]$

$w_1 = b$. The edges b and a together are still acyclic so

$E = [a, b]$

$w_2 = c$. The edge with those in E make a cycle so c cannot be added

$E = [a, b]$

$w_3 = d$. The edge d with those in E are still acyclic

$E = [a, b, d]$

$w_4 = e$. The edge e with those in E are still acyclic

$E = [a, b, d, e]$

$w_5 = f$. The edge f with those in E would create a cycle and so the final list is

$E = [a, b, d, e]$

Traversing trees

There are a number of general algorithms for traversing graphs (moving from one node to another node) but we are going to restrict our study to traversing trees. Specifically, we shall look at two types of tree traversal: 'preorder' and 'postorder'. For examples we shall use the tree in Figure 7.21.

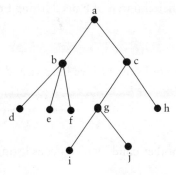

Figure 7.21   Tree used to illustrate preorder and postorder traversal.

The different algorithms determine when the root of a tree is visited in comparison to subtrees. For preorder the root is listed first and the subtrees are listed in the order of their roots. The order taken is left to right. So, in our example tree the root is a.

    a

The next two subtrees have roots b and c but b is to the left of c and so we explore the subtrees of b.

    a b

Each child of b is a leaf node and so we add each child in left to right order

    a b d e f

Next we have c

    a b d e f c

the left child of c is g and so we explore the children of g

    a b d e f c g

Each child of g is a leaf node so we add them in order

    a b d e f c g i j

finally we add h to give the full preorder listing

    a b d e f c g i j h

For postorder listing, the subtrees are listed in order first and finally the root. So for our example we start with the left-most leaf which is d

    d

The root for d is b but the other children of b need listing first

    d e f b

The root for b is a but we cannot list a until we have visited the subtrees of c.
The left-most leaf from the root c is i

    d e f b i

The root of i is g but g has another child j which needs listing first

    d e f b i j g

The root of g is c but before c can be listed we need to finish all subtrees. The only
leaf not explored yet is h

    d e f b i j g h

and finally we can add c then a to get the full postorder listing

    d e f b i j g h c a

The algorithms presented next take advantage of the recursive nature of trees. The
algorithms are recursive algorithms which means that they have a line that refers back
to the algorithm. An example should make things clear.

Preorder algorithm

We start with a tree T that has a list of subtrees $T_1, T_2, \ldots T_n$ in left to
right order. We shall use r to refer to a tree's root. The preorder
algorithm is called with a tree and so it shall take a single argument of
type tree.

     Preorder(T)

     print r
     for $i = 0$ to less than n (number of subtrees)
       Preorder (T_i)

Example 7.11

List the order of node visits for a preorder traversal of the tree in Figure 7.21.

Solution
We shall use T_r to denote the tree whose root is r. So we start with $r = a$ and a has
two subtrees T_b and T_c

print a
For T_b and T_c
   Preorder (T_b)
     print b
     for T_d, T_e and T_f (subtrees of b)
       Preorder(T_d)
         print d   no subtrees of d so we return back from the last call
       Preorder(T_e)
         print e   no subtrees of e so we return back from the last call
       Preorder(T_f)
         print f   no subtrees of f so we return back from the last call
   Preorder (T_c)
     print c
     for T_g and T_h (subtrees of c)
     Preorder(T_g)
       print g
       for T_i and T_j (subtrees of g)
       Preorder (T_i)
         print i   no subtrees of i and so we return from the last call
       Preorder (T_j)
         print j   no subtrees of j and so we return from the last call
     Preorder(T_h)
       write h   no subtrees of h

The algorithm has no outstanding calls to make. If we write the list of nodes out in the order they were printed we get:

   a b d e f c g i j h

Postorder algorithm

Postorder(T)
For $i = 0$ to less than n
      Postorder (T_i)
Print r

Example 7.12

List the order of node visits for a postorder traversal of the tree in Figure 7.21.

Solution
Postorder (T_a)
For T_b and T_c
   Postorder(T_b)
   For T_d, T_e and T_f (subtrees of b)
     Postorder(T_d)
     (there are no children of d and so we have no for loop)
     print d
     Postorder(T_e)
     (there are no children of e and so we have no for loop)

    print e
    Postorder(T_f)
    (there are no children of f and so we have no for loop)
    print f
print b (the loop for Postorder(T_b) has completed)
Postorder(T_c)
For T_g and T_h
    Postorder(T_g)
    For T_i and T_j
        Postorder(T_i)
        (there are no children of i and so we have no for loop)
        print i
        Postorder(T_j)
        (there are no children of j and so we have no for loop)
        print j
    print g (finished with the loop for T_g)
    Postorder(T_h)
    (there are no children of h and so we have no for loop)
    print h
(we have now finished with the loop for c)
print c
(we have now finished with the loop for a)
print a
Listing the nodes in order of printing we get:
    d e f b i j g h c a

A tree that has two children for every internal node is called a binary tree. A third kind of listing exists for binary trees called an 'inorder' listing.

7.3

Answers appear in Appendix A.

1 Sketch two spanning trees for the graph in Figure 7.22.

2 Use Kruskal's algorithm to find a minimum spanning tree for Figure 7.22.

3 List the order of node visits for a preorder and postorder traversal of Figure 7.23.

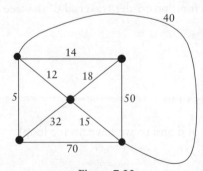

Figure 7.22

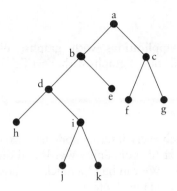

Figure 7.23

Summary

A graph is a non-empty set of vertices and edges. An edge has two vertices as endpoints. Two vertices that act as the endpoints of an edge are said to be adjacent. An edge that has the same vertex for both endpoints is a loop. Two edges that have the same endpoints are parallel edges. A simple graph has no loops or parallel edges. The degree of a vertex is the number of edges that meet at that vertex; a loop adds degree 2 to the vertex.

A path is a sequence of node visits separated by the edge traversed between a node and the succeeding node in the sequence. The length of a path is the number of edges it contains. A connected graph has a path from any vertex to any other vertex. Where a path starts and finishes at the same vertex, with no vertex other than the start vertex occurring more than once, and no edge occurring more than once, the path is called a cycle. An acyclic graph is one with no cycles. An acyclic graph is a simple graph.

A directed graph defines in which direction an edge can be traversed. A labelled graph has the vertices labelled and a weighted graph associates each edge with a numerical value.

A graph can be represented using an adjacency matrix which is an $n \times n$ matrix for a graph with n nodes.

An Euler path traverses every edge of a graph exactly once. Fleury's algorithm can be used to find an Euler path.

A tree is a connected graph with no cycles. An internal node (vertex) has child nodes and a leaf node has no child nodes. The depth of a node is the length of the path from the root node to the node and the height of a tree is the maximum depth of any node.

A spanning tree is a subgraph of a graph G that contains all the vertices in G and is a tree. A minimum spanning tree is the spanning tree with the lowest total weight (sum of all weights) for a weighted graph. Kruskal's algorithm can be used to find a minimum spanning tree.

Preorder and postorder are tree traversal algorithms. For preorder the root is listed first and the subtrees are listed in the order (left to right) of their roots. For postorder listing, the subtrees are listed in order first and finally the root.

Applications

We shall consider three applications with graphs; binary search, Huffman compression, and the general role of graphs within artificial intelligence.

Binary tree search

A binary tree is a tree in which every internal node has two child nodes. Suppose we want to be able to open a text file containing words and once the file is read to tell quickly if a word is in the file. We can build a quick method of searching by using a binary tree. Suppose the file contains the text:

'Today is a wonderful day for cricket'

We take the first word 'Today' and make it a label for the root of a tree. We generate two child nodes for the tree (left and right). The second word 'is' comes before the word 'Today' according to the alphabet and so we label the left child node as 'is' and generate two child nodes for 'is'. The third word 'a' comes before 'Today' and so we take the left branch to 'is'. Since 'a' comes before 'is' we label the left child of 'is' with 'a' and generate two child nodes for 'a'. The word 'wonderful' comes after 'Today' and it becomes the label for the right child of 'Today'. We proceed in this fashion taking a left branch when the word we are placing comes before the label of the current node or the right node if it is after. Any word appears only once in the tree. The tree is built up as shown in Figure 7.24.

Once the tree is built the search for a word is quick and easy. We start at the root node and inspect the node's label. If it is not the word we are looking for we take the left branch if our word comes before the label of the node and the right branch if after. This process is repeated until either the word is found or a leaf node is reached (in which case the word is not in the tree). If the words are listed by starting at the root node, listing the left child first, then the node, then the right child, the output is:

a cricket day for is today wonderful.

Huffman compression

Huffman compression is a simple technique for saving storage space with text files. In a computer, characters are represented as binary strings and it is typical to represent each character of the alphabet using 8 bits. If for example, a file contains the sequence 'AAAAABBBCCC', the storage required is 88 bits. If on the other hand, 'A' were to be represented using only 1 bit and both 'B' and 'C' with two bits, the storage required would fall to 17 bits. Imagine that 1 represents 'A' and 00 a 'B' and 01 a C, the string is then represented as

1 1 1 1 1 00 00 00 01 01 01

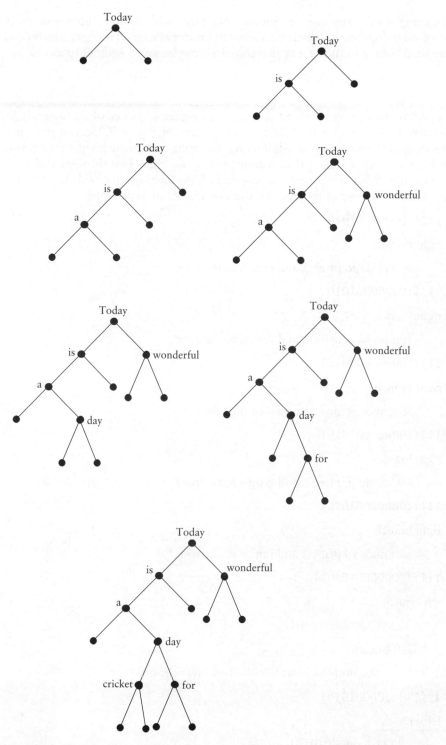

Figure 7.24 The generation of a binary search tree for 'Today is a good day for cricket'.

This string is still expensive on storage since each blank space occupies storage. We have used the spaces to delimit (i.e., separate) the characters. However, the bit codes have been chosen in such a way that the string can be saved without spaces as

11111000000010101

How can this string be decoded to get the original sequence of characters if each character is not delimited? Well, look at the tree in Figure 7.25. You start at the beginning of the bit string and shift along this string by a single bit at a time taking a left branch every a time a 0 is encountered and a right branch every time a 1 is encountered. When a leaf node is encountered, the label for that node is printed and we return to the root of the tree. So, the example string is decoded as:

<u>1</u>1111000000010101

right branch

    leaf node so print A and return to the root

1<u>1</u>111000000010101

right branch

    leaf node so print A and return to the root

11<u>1</u>11000000010101

right branch

    leaf node so print A and return to the root

111<u>1</u>1000000010101

right branch

    leaf node so print A and return to the root

1111<u>1</u>000000010101

right branch

    leaf node so print A and return to the root

11111<u>0</u>00000010101

left branch

    111110<u>0</u>0000010101

    left branch

        leaf node so print B and return to the root

111110<u>0</u>0000010101

left branch

    1111100<u>0</u>000010101

left branch

leaf node so print B and return to the root

1111100000<u>0</u>0010101

left branch

1111100000<u>0</u>0010101

left branch

leaf node so print B and return to the root

111110000000<u>0</u>10101

left branch

1111100000001<u>0</u>101

right branch

leaf node so print C and return to the root

11111000000010<u>1</u>01

left branch

1111100000001<u>0</u>101

right branch

leaf node so print C and return to the root

1111100000001<u>0</u>1

left branch

11111000000010<u>1</u>01

right branch

leaf node so print C and return to the root

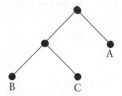

Figure 7.25   A tree for generating Huffman codes.

Huffman coding provides the algorithm for constructing the tree of codes. Storage is saved by assigning the shortest bit codes to the most frequently occurring characters. In our example the character 'A' occurs most frequently and hence it had the shortest code of a single character.

The Huffman algorithm is:

1. Count the frequency of each character in the file. Each character needs a leaf node and so create a list of leaf nodes. The leaf node stores the character and its frequency count.

2. While the list of nodes is not empty
   (a) Create a parent node (an internal node)
   (b) Select the two nodes with the lowest frequency
   (c) Attach the selected nodes as child nodes to the parent node in left to right order
   (d) Sum the frequency count of each child node and assign this count to the parent node
   (e) Add the parent node to the list.

3. Traverse the tree and assign the bit codes to each leaf node.

Example

Let us generate the tree for

> Today is a good day for cricket

The frequency count is

> {(A, 3), (C, 2), (D, 3), (E, 1), (F, 1), (G, 1), (I, 2), (K, 1), (O, 4), (R, 2), (S, 1), (T, 2), (Y, 2)}

We shall label internal node as N1, N2, N3, etc.

Any of the characters with a frequency of 1 can be selected first. We shall select E and F and create the parent node N1. We shall denote the children of each parent node using a triple of the form (parent, left child, right child). So we have

> (N1, E, F)

and the frequency for N1 is $1 + 1$. So the list is now:

> {(A, 3), (C, 2), (D, 3), (G, 1), (I, 2), (K, 1), (O, 4), (R, 2), (S, 1), (T, 2), (Y, 2), (N1, 2)}

This process is repeated until the list is empty.

> (N2, G, K)
>
> {(A, 3), (C, 2), (D, 3), (I, 2), (O, 4), (R, 2), (S, 1), (T, 2), (Y, 2), (N1, 2), (N2, 2)}
>
> (N3, S, I)
>
> {(A, 3), (C, 2), (D, 3), (O, 4), (R, 2), (T, 2), (Y, 2), (N1, 2), (N2, 2), (N3, 3)}

(N4, C, R)

{(A, 3), (D, 3), (O, 4), (T, 2), (Y, 2), (N1, 2), (N2, 2), (N3, 3), (N4, 4)}

(N5, T, Y)

{(A, 3), (D, 3), (O, 4), (N1, 2), (N2, 2), (N3, 3), (N4, 4), (N5, 4)}

(N6, N1, N2)

{(A, 3), (D, 3), (O, 4), (N3, 3), (N4, 4), (N5, 4), (N6, 4)}

(N7, A, D)

{(O, 4), (N3, 3), (N4, 4), (N5, 4), (N6, 4), (N7, 6)}

(N8, N3, O)

{(N4, 4), (N5, 4), (N6, 4), (N7, 6), (N8, 7)}

(N9, N4, N5)

{(N6, 4), (N7, 6), (N8, 7), (N9, 8)}

(N10, N6, N7)

{(N8, 7), (N9, 8), (N10, 10)}

(N11, N8, N9)

{(N10, 10), (N11, 15)}

(N12, N10, N11)

The tree is given in Figure 7.26.

Computing in artificial intelligence

Artificial intelligence (AI) is the study of techniques to get a machine to perform tasks that humans are good at but are difficult to program using more conventional techniques. These tasks might involve low-level tasks such as image recognition or higher-level tasks such as natural language processing or robot planning. Graphs are used in many ways within AI for the representation of knowledge and searching graphs is a fundamental part of many AI systems. During the early years of AI, the late 1950s and early 1960s, researchers concentrated on small puzzles with which they explored ideas. A puzzle might involve a planning task such as reordering a stack of coloured blocks. The solution to the block-stacking task can be represented with tree searching. The root node is used to denote the start-state which is the initial configuration of the blocks. Each branch represents a move. The moves that can be made depend on the capability of the robot. The robot might be restricted to moving one block at a time or it might be able to move two at a time. Each node in the tree represents a state (configuration of the blocks) and the planning task is to find the goal-state. For instance the goal might be to get a red block on top of the blue block and the blue block on top of the green. You can probably appreciate that there is

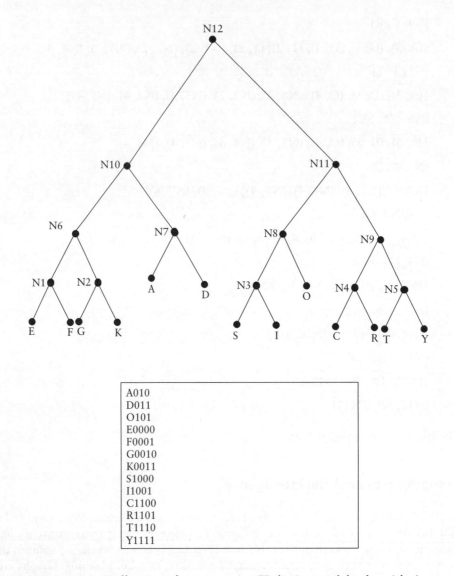

A010
D011
O101
E0000
F0001
G0010
K0011
S1000
I1001
C1100
R1101
T1110
Y1111

Figure 7.26   Huffman tree for compressing 'Today is a good day for cricket'.

usually more than one way of solving a task and so we would expect to see the goal-state appear at more than one node. A goal-state with the least depth (nearest the root of the tree) represents the shortest number of moves to get to the goal-state. The challenge for building search algorithms is to find the most efficient way of solving a task. An example tree is given in Figure 7.27.

Small puzzles can be searched exhaustively for a solution because the search space (the tree that represents all possible states) is small. However, interesting problems and real-world problems have huge search spaces. For example, the game of chess

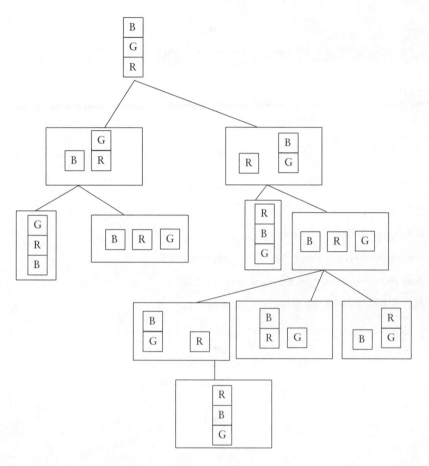

Figure 7.27 Part of a search space that is generated when stacking the blocks with blue on top of green and red on top of blue.

has a search space with approximately 10^{120} states. For real-world problems you cannot expect to search the whole space and so it is usual to use knowledge of the task to perform what is called heuristic searching. An experienced chess player will have many more heuristics (rules of thumb) than a novice player.

EXERCISES

Answers appear in Appendix B.

1 For the graph in Figure 7.28
  (a) Give the degree of vertices 2 and 5
  (b) Give the adjacency matrix
  (c) The matrix of paths of length 2
  (d) The matrix of paths of length 3

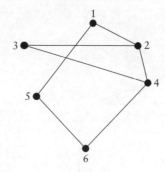

Figure 7.28

2   Is the graph in Figure 7.28 simple?

3   Starting at vertex 5 in Figure 7.28 give a cycle of length 6

4   Does an Euler path exist for the graph in Figure 7.28?

5   Give an Euler path for the graph in Figure 7.29

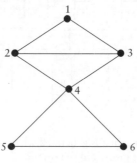

Figure 7.29

6   Give an Euler path for the graph in Figure 7.30

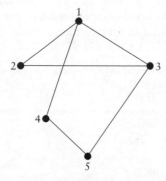

Figure 7.30

7 For the tree in Figure 7.31
   (a) Give the height of the tree
   (b) Give the depth of node g
   (c) Give the depth of node n

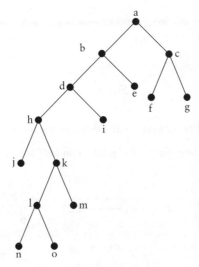

Figure 7.31

8 Give the list of leaf nodes (the tree in bracket notation) for the subtree with d as its root in Figure 7.31.

9 How many subtrees are there in Figure 7.31?

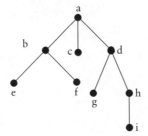

Figure 7.32

10 Give the preorder listing of node visits for the tree in Figure 7.32.

11 Give the postorder listing of node visits for the tree in Figure 7.32.

12 Give the preorder listing of node visits for the tree in Figure 7.31.

13 Give the postorder listing of node visits for the tree in Figure 7.31.

14 Find the minimum spanning tree for the graph in Figure 7.33.

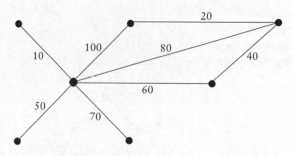

Figure 7.33

15 Give another spanning tree for Figure 7.33 other than the minimum spanning tree.

16 Find the minimum spanning tree for the graph in Figure 7.34.

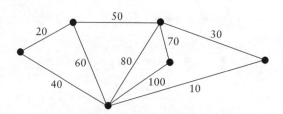

Figure 7.34

8

Counting, probability and fuzzy systems

Introduction

Probability has many applications, from the quality control of manufacturing output to machine learning algorithms (algorithms that permit a machine to learn a task without being programmed in a conventional way). In order to estimate probabilities we need to know how to count the members of a set and so this chapter starts with an introduction to the different ways in which objects can be selected from a set and how to count the selected objects. This is followed by an introduction to elementary probability which you might remember from school. The section on probability concludes with a look at Bayes' rule which has proved to be extremely useful for many applications. The last section looks at 'fuzzy systems' which is the study of reasoning with vague (fuzzy) knowledge as opposed to the clear-cut black and white logic that we studied in Chapters 1 and 3. There are a number of places where this section of the book could be placed. It might have been positioned in the chapters on logic since fuzzy systems deal with fuzzy logic or with the chapter on sets because we have fuzzy sets or perhaps with the chapter on relations. Since fuzzy systems rely on the mathematics of all those chapters it seemed appropriate to position it after the material on logic, sets and relations. Another reason for choosing this chapter to present fuzzy systems is because the subject is related to probability in that both find a role in handling uncertainty.

Combinations

Let us consider the set of characters {a, b, c} and see in what way we can make up strings that have two characters like ab or bc, etc. We can use rules to allow four types of combination.

- Rule1: Allow a character to be repeated, and order matters, which means that the string ab is different to ba. To form the strings we shall take each character in turn and combine it with every character in the set. So, starting with a

    aa ab ac

With b

    ba bb bc

With c

    ca cb cc

The complete list using our first rule is

    aa, ab, ac, ba, bb, bc, ca, cb, cc

- Rule 2: Do not allow a character to be repeated but order matters. We get the list for this rule if we take our first list and remove strings with repeated characters:

    ab, ac, ba, bc, ca, cb

- Rule 3: Allow repeated characters but order does not matter which means that a string like ab is the same as ba. Again we can take the listing from the first rule and cancel strings that do not satisfy the rule. The listing is:

    aa, ab, ac, ba, bb, bc, ca, cb, cc

Looking through the list, aa can be kept because repeated characters are allowed. The second string ab can be kept but we need to eliminate ba because this is considered the same string. If we do likewise for the other remaining strings we get our final list:

    aa, ab, ac, bb, bc, cc

- Rule 4: Do not allow repeated characters and order does not matter. We can use the listing from Rule 3 and remove strings with repeating characters:

    ab, ac, bc

Our four rules have outlined four basic ways in which we can combine objects taken from a set. The basic ways are:

- ordered selection with repetition
- ordered selection without repetition
- unordered selection with repetition
- unordered selection without repetition.

These basic ways of making a selection occur frequently in problems. For example, if you wanted to issue a six-digit personal identification number to members of a bank and the numbers are to be made up from the digits 0–9 you would have an ordered selection with repetition. Order matters because the string 345278 is different from 784325 even though both contain the same digits. Repetition is allowed because you can have repeated digits. If, on the other hand, you wanted to select a football team from a class of students without any concern for the position a student is to play, order does not matter and repetition is not allowed. Order does not matter because if you were to line up your players after selection and then get them to swap positions in the line you would still have the same team. If, though, you were to assign your players to playing positions when you make the selection, then order would matter because now you can line up the players according to the position they play. Repetition does not count for our team because you cannot select the same player twice.

Example 8.1

Given the set of people {John, David, Sara, Debbie} write down the selections that can be made to form a committee of two people.

Solution

John, David

John, Sara

John, Debbie

David, Sara (David, John is the same as John, David)

David, Debbie

Sara, Debbie

In this problem order does not matter and repetition is not allowed.

Example 8.2

Given the set of people {John, David, Sara, Debbie} write down the selections that can be made to form a committee of two people with one member as the chair.

Solution
We shall note the chair by putting placing a C after their name.

John C, David

John C, Sara

John C, Debbie

David C, John (David, John is different John, David because the role of chair has changed)

David C, Sara

David C, Debbie

Sara C, John

Sara C, David

Sara C, Debbie

Debbie C, John

Debbie C, David

Debbie C, Sara

This time, order matters.

Example 8.3

A company is to issue three-digit telephone extensions to all staff but they can only select extensions from the digits $\{1, 2, 3\}$. Write down all possible combinations.

Solution
Digits can be repeated and the order matters.

111	211	311
112	212	312
113	213	313
121	221	321
122	222	322
123	223	323
131	231	331
132	232	332
133	233	333

So there are 27 possible extensions.

Addition principle

If k disjoint subsets can be formed from a set of objects with n_i objects in subset i then we get $n_1 + n_2 + \dots + n_k$ objects all together.

Disjoint means that each subset is considered to contain different objects.

Example 8.4

You are in an Indian restaurant and the menu offers three Korma dishes, five Tikka dishes, and four Balti dishes. How many selections are available?

Solution
Each type of dish forms a disjoint subset. For instance, a chicken Korma is a different dish from a chicken Tikka. Using the addition principle we get 12 selections – the sum of dishes in each of the three sets.

Example 8.5

A University has six Faculties with 30, 20, 50, 35, 12, and 40 lecturers in each Faculty. The board of governors needs a lecturer representative. How many possible representatives are there?

Solution
Again by the addition principle there 187 potential representatives.

> **Multiplication principle**
>
> If there are n_i possible outcomes for event i, and there are k events, then there are $n_1 \times n_2 \times \ldots \times n_k$ possible outcomes for the sequence of events.

Example 8.6

You are holding auditions to form a rock group and you need to select one guitar player from six guitarists, one drummer from three drummers and one singer from eight singers. How many different possible groups are there?

Solution
We can select a guitar player from six and for each guitar player we can select one of the drummers to give 6×3 possible groups with one guitar player and one drummer. Each one of these groups can then be combined with a singer and so there are $6 \times 3 \times 8 = 144$ possible groups. We have just applied the multiplication principle.

Example 8.7

Your friend has left you in charge of her pie shop. She tells you that all pies are sold either with chips or a jacket potato. There are four different pies. How many different sale combinations are there?

Solution
Let us label the pies as pie1, pie2, etc. Then pie1 can be sold with either chips or jacket potato, so too can pie2, pie3 and pie4. So there are $4 \times 2 = 8$ possible sale combinations.

Ordered selection with repetition

We have the set of characters {a, b, c} and we want to see how many strings of length two we can make. The selection is ordered and repetition is allowed. Repetition means that after we have selected the first character from the set we put it back. So for the first character we have a choice of three. If we replace the first character we still have a choice of three and so the total selections is $3 \times 3 = 9$.

If we wanted strings of length three from the set {a, b, c} we would have $3 \times 3 \times 3 = 27$ or 3^3 selections.

> The number of ordered selections of k objects with repetition from a set
> of n objects is n^k.

Example 8.8

How many personal identification numbers of six digits can a bank issue using the
digits 0–9?

Solution
We have an ordered selection with repetition. We have a set of ten objects from
which we wish to select six and so there are 10^6 selections.

Example 8.9

How many three-letter strings can be generated from the string of letters BRAIN?
Note that a string does not have to be a sensible word – it might, for example, contain
only consonants.

Solution
We want a selection of three characters from five and so there are 5^3 possible strings.

Example 8.10

How many strings of length three can you make from the set {0, 1}?

Solution
Again, we have an ordered selection with repetition. We want to select three objects
from a set of two and so there are 2^3 possible strings.

Ordered selection without repetition

We have the set of characters {a, b, c} and we want to see how many strings of length
two we can make without any character being repeated. The selection is ordered and
repetition is not allowed. No repetition means that after we have selected the first
character from the set we do not put it back. So for the first character we have a
choice of three. If we do not replace the first character we have a choice of two for
the second and so the total number of strings is $3 \times 2 = 6$.

> The number of ordered selections of k objects without repetition from a
> set of n objects is $n \times (n - 1) \times (n - 2) \ldots (n - k + 1)$ denoted by $P(n, k)$

We can express $P(n, k)$ using the definition of n factorial denoted by $n!$. The definition of n factorial is $n \times (n - 1) \times (n - 2) \ldots (1)$ and so $5!$ is $5 \times 4 \times 3 \times 2 \times 1 = 120$ and $3!$ is $3 \times 2 \times 1 = 6$. Using the definition of n factorial we can write

$$P(n, k) = \frac{n!}{(n - k)!}$$

So,

$$P(10,4) = \frac{10!}{(10 - 4)!} = \frac{10!}{6!} = \frac{10 \cdot 9 \cdot 8 \cdot 7 \cdot 6 \cdot 5 \cdot 4 \cdot 3 \cdot 2 \cdot 1}{6 \cdot 5 \cdot 4 \cdot 3 \cdot 2 \cdot 1} = 5040$$

Example 8.11

How many three-letter strings can be generated from the string of letters BRAIN if no letter can be repeated?

Solution
We have an ordered selection because BIN is different from NIB. Repetition is not allowed and so we need to calculate $P(5,3)$.

$$P(5,3) = \frac{5!}{(5 - 3)!} - \frac{5 \cdot 4 \cdot 3 \cdot 2 \cdot 1}{2 \cdot 1} = 60$$

Example 8.12

We need to select a chairman, treasurer and secretary for a tennis club from the players. There are 20 players. How many selections can be made?

Solution
Again, order matters and we cannot have repetition because the same person cannot perform two roles. So we have

$$P(20,3) = \frac{20!}{17!} = 6840$$

Example 8.13

There are six parking spaces on a garage forecourt. In how many ways can six cars be displayed on the forecourt?

Solution
Again, we have an ordered selection without repetition (a car cannot park in two places at the same time). So we have

$$P(6,6) = \frac{6!}{0!} = 720$$

Unordered selection without repetition

It is easier to deal first with unordered selections without repetition and then deal with the case where repetition is allowed.

We have the set of characters {a, b, c} and we want to see how many unordered strings of length two we can make without any character being repeated. Remember that unordered means that the string ab is considered to be the same as ba. We noted at the start of this section that the list of unordered selections without repetition is

ab, ac, bc

> The number of unordered selections of k objects without repetition from a set of n objects is $\dfrac{n!}{k!(n-k)!}$ denoted by $\dbinom{n}{k}$ or $C(n, k)$

This type of selection is called a 'combination'. We see that the formula is closely related to that for a permutation. To see the relationship let us consider again Example 8.12:

We need to select a chairman, treasurer and secretary for a tennis club from the players. There are 20 players. How many selections can be made?

Let us see how many ways we can select three committee members without any concern for the roles of chairman, treasurer or secretary. So we have

$$\binom{20}{3} = \frac{20!}{3! \times 17!} = 1140$$

Let us imagine that the three selected players are: Sue, Debbie and George. If we write these players down in order of chairman, treasurer and secretary the combinations are

Sue Debbie George

Sue George Debbie

Debbie Sue George

Debbie George Sue

George Debbie Sue

George Sue Debbie

So we have six or 3! orders. So each combination could be ordered in 3! ways. This leads to

$C(n, k).k! = P(n, k)$

1140 times 3! gives 6840, the result we had for Example 8.12.

Example 8.14

In how many ways can eight cards be selected from a 52-card set?

Solution
Order does not matter here. For instance, if you lay the eight cards out on a table and rearrange them into a different sequence you still have the same selection. Repetition is not allowed because no card is repeated. So we have

$$\binom{52}{8} = \frac{52!}{8! \times 44!}$$

Example 8.15

You wish to select a committee of four from 20 first-year students and 30 second-year students. You must have two from each year. How many combinations are there?

Solution
Order does not matter and we have no repetition. We know we have to select two students from each year. So for the first year we have $\binom{20}{2}$ and for the second $\binom{30}{2}$.

We now use the multiplication principle and get $\binom{20}{2} \times \binom{30}{2}$.

Example 8.16

A tyre manufacturer produces 1000 tyres a day of which 5% need to be tested for quality control. How many ways can this test be done?

Solution
Order does not matter and you cannot select the same tyre more than once and so there is no repetition. The number of tyres tested is 50. The answer then is $\binom{1000}{50}$.

Unordered selection with repetition

We have the set of characters {a, b, c} and we want to see how many unordered strings of length two we can make with allowing repeating characters. The list is

aa, ab, ac, bb, bc, cc

Let us look at another example. Four people are in an Italian restaurant and they have decided to order four pizzas and share them. The menu has three types of pizza. How many selections are there? A typical way of explaining the solution is to use an order form which has three columns, one for each type of pizza.

Pizza 1	Pizza 2	Pizza 3
xx	x	x

We have an unordered selection because all pizzas will be shared. Also we can have repeats; indeed, we need to have one repeat otherwise we cannot have four pizzas! If we look at the second row on the order form we can imagine it as a string as follows:

xx | x | x

We can create strings for other orders like

xx | xx |

| xxxx |

x | x | xx

...

Any sequence of the six xs and two |s is a unique selection. The whole string is composed of six characters and we can change the order by simply moving the |s. So our problem is to select two positions (for the |s) from six available which is $\binom{6}{4}$.

> The number of unordered selections of k objects with repetition from a set of n objects is $\binom{n+k-1}{k}$ or $C(n+k-1, k)$

So for the pizza problem we have $n = 3$ and $k = 4$.

Example 8.17

You have to purchase six bicycles for your cycle hire business and the shop has eight different models available. How many selections can you make?

Solution
This is an unordered selection and you can repeat any choice (if we assume the shop has six of each type in stock). So the number of selections is $\binom{8+6-1}{6}$ or 1716 selections.

Example 8.18

You have ten record vouchers to distribute amongst 30 customers. A single customer is allowed to have any number of vouchers so you could decide to award one massive gift and give all 30 to one customer. How many ways can the vouchers be distributed?

Solution
We have an unordered selection with repetition. Think of each customer as occupying a column (on our order form) and we have to place zero, one or more vouchers in each column. The number of distributions is

$$\binom{30 + 10 - 1}{10}$$

8.1

Answers appear in Appendix A.

1 Calculate (a) 4! (b) 8!

2 Calculate (a) $P(5, 4)$ (b) $P(12, 2)$ (c) $P(7, 6)$ (d) $P(3, 2)$ (e) $P(3, 3)$

3 Calculate (a) $\binom{30}{6}$ (b) $\binom{10}{8}$ (c) $\binom{3}{3}$

For the following questions think carefully about whether the selection is ordered or unordered and whether repetition is allowed.

4 A tennis club has ten competitive players. In how many ways can a team of four players be selected if
   (a) the team players have to be ranked in capability
   (b) the team players do not need to be ranked.

5 There are ten football teams in a league table and each team is ranked. How many possible orderings of the table are there?

6 How many ways can you select a committee of four people from 15?

7 How many ways can you select a chairman and secretary from 20 people?

8 You are in a restaurant and you need to select a starter and main course from a selection of twelve dishes. How many selections can you make?

Binomial theorem

The number $\binom{n}{k}$ is known as the 'binomial coefficient' and in this section we shall see why. Let us look at the expansion of $(a + b)^2$. We can expand term by term:

$$(a + b)(a + b) = aa + ab + ba + bb$$
$$= a^2 + 2ab + b^2$$

Consider the expansion of $(a + b)^3$

$$(a + b)^3 = (a + b)(a + b)(a + b)$$
$$= aa^2 + ba^2 + 2a^2b + 2ab^2 + ab^2 + b^3$$
$$= a^3 + 3a^2b + 3ab^2 + b^3$$

Note that here *a* and *b* are real numbers and so the product *ab* is the same as *ba*.

> The binomial theorem for real values a and b, and positive integer n states:
>
> $$(a + b)^n = \binom{n}{0} a^n b^0 + \binom{n}{1} a^{n-1} b^1 + \binom{n}{2} a^{n-2} b^2 + \dots + \binom{n}{n} a^0 b^n$$

We can see that $\binom{n}{k}$ corresponds to the coefficients in the expansion of $(a + b)^n$.

Example 8.19

Give the coefficient of x^3 in the expansion of $(1 + x)^4$.

Solution
We have $a = 1$ and $b = x$ and $n = 4$. We want the coefficient for b^3 which according to the theorem is

$$\binom{n}{3} \text{ or } \binom{4}{3}$$

Example 8.20

Calculate

$$\binom{3}{0} + \binom{3}{1} + \binom{3}{2} + \binom{3}{3}$$

using the binomial theorem.

Solution
We know from the binomial theorem that

$$(1 + 1)^3 = \binom{3}{0} 1^3 1^0 + \binom{3}{1} 1^2 1^1 + \binom{3}{2} 1^1 1^2 + \binom{3}{3} 1^0 1^3$$

So

$$(1 + 1)^3 = \binom{3}{0} + \binom{3}{1} + \binom{3}{2} + \binom{3}{3}$$

which gives 2^3.

8.2

Answers appear in Appendix A.

1 Give the coefficients of x^3 and x^5 in the expansion of $(1 + x)^5$.

2 Use the binomial theorem to evaluate $\binom{2}{0} + \binom{2}{1} + \binom{2}{2}$

Probability

We are going to start this section with a review of elementary probability that you have most likely met before.

Basic rules of probability

If you flip a coin there are two possible outcomes: the coin could land on heads (H) or on tails (T). So the set of outcomes is {H, T}. The set of outcomes is called a 'sample space'. Suppose we flip a coin and then flip it again; the possible outcomes are:

{HH, HT, TH, TT}

We might be interested in calculating the likelihood (i.e., chance) of getting HH (head followed by a head). We might be interested in calculating the probability of HT or TH. Each of these possible results that we are interested in is an 'event' and each event is a subset of the sample space. The probability of an event is a number in the range 0–1. If our coin is unbiased (fair) then we would expect the coin to land as many times on heads as it does tails. For a single flip of an unbiased coin there are two events (outcome heads or outcome tails) and both events are equally likely.

We can perform an experiment to see if a coin is unbiased. We could flip the coin a number of times and see how many times it lands on heads and how many times it lands on tails. The probability that it lands on heads is then estimated by taking the ratio of the total number of times the coin landed on heads to the total number of flips. How many times should we flip the coin? How about ten flips? I flipped a coin ten times just before writing this sentence and found that it landed on tails seven out of the ten flips. Is the coin biased? Well, if I flipped the coin a 100 times or better still 500 times I would expect to get a better estimate. You have to be cautious when measuring probabilities. It is unlikely, but possible, that in an experiment of flipping an unbiased coin 100 times the coin actually lands on heads 100 times. If we flip the coin a 1000 times the chance of it landing every time on heads is a lot lower than for the coin landing on heads every time on 100 flips. The more times we flip the coin the closer we get to estimating its probability for the event of landing on heads or tails.

Usually we take a coin to be unbiased and therefore the probability of it landing on heads is the same as landing on tails. The probability of an event E is written as

P(E)

So the probability of heads (H) is

$P(H) = \frac{1}{2}$

And tails

$P(T) = \frac{1}{2}$

The probability of all events from our sample space must add to 1. So we see that P(H) + P(T) is 1.

For a fair dice (see Figure 8.1), the probability of it landing on 1 is

$$P(1) - 1/6$$

The probability is also 1/6 for P(2), P(3), P(4), P(5) and P(6).

Figure 8.1   Two dice

The sample space for the dice is {1, 2, 3, 4, 5, 6}. Each event has a probability of 1/6 and the sum of all events is 1. A friend has offered you ten pounds if you throw a 2 or a 6 on a throw of a fair dice. We are interested in the event E = {2, 6}. The probability of this event is

$$P(E) = 1/6 + 1/6 = 1/3.$$

What is the probability of not getting a 3 on the throw of a fair dice? The probability of not getting a 3 is the event E = {1, 2, 4, 5, 6} = 5/6. Note that from set theory the complement of E in this case is E^c = {3}: the probability of getting a 3. Note that

$$P(E) + P(E^c) = 1$$

Suppose our friend says he will offer us ten pounds if we throw either a 2 or a 6, or an even number. We now have events E = {2, 6} and 'even number' F = {2, 4, 6}. What is the probability of winning the ten pounds? We win on the event G = {2, 4, 6} and so the probability of winning is $1/6 + 1/6 + 1/6 = \frac{1}{2}$. Note that G is the union of E and F. Can we estimate P(G) from P(E) and P(F)? We have P(E) = 1/3 and P(F) = $\frac{1}{2}$ and P(E) + P(F) = 5/6. When we calculated P(E) + P(F) we took {2, 6} into account twice because {2, 6} is a subset of both E and F. So we need to subtract P({2, 6}) to get 5/6 − 1/3 = 1/2. Note that event {2, 6} is $P(E \cap F) = \frac{1}{3}$.

Our friend is now offering fifty pounds if we can throw two 3s in succession. What is the probability of winning the fifty pounds with a fair dice? Say we throw a 1 on the first throw. For the second throw we can still get one of six numbers. Writing down the sequence as an ordered pair where a 1 is thrown first we have:

$$(1, 1), (1, 2), (1, 3), (1, 4), (1, 5), (1, 6).$$

Suppose now we throw a 2 on the first throw:

$$(2, 1), (2, 2), (2, 3), (2, 4), (2, 5), (2, 6).$$

If we repeat this for 3, 4, 5 and 6 on the first throw we see that our sample space has 36 possible outcomes. Only for one of these (3, 3) do we win fifty pounds. So the

$$P(\{(3, 3)\}) = 1/36$$

We can also observe that it is the product of the probability of throwing 3 on this first throw with throwing 3 on the second:

$$P(\{3\}) \cdot P(\{3\}) = 1/6 \times 1/6 = 1/36.$$

Now that we have seen some examples we can state some basic rules of probability.

> (a) The sum of all event probabilities drawn from a sample space add to 1
> (b) $P(E^C) = 1 - P(E)$ for event E
> (c) $P(E_1 \cup E_2) = P(E_1) + P(E_2) - P(E_1 \cap E_2)$ for events E_1 and E_2. This is the probability of event E_1 or E_2. Either E_1 occurs or E_2 occurs or both.
>
> Note that we also use $P(E_1 \cap E_2)$ to denote that events E_1 and E_2 both occur.

Example 8.21

An unbiased coin is flipped four times in succession. What is the probability of the coin landing three or more times on heads?

Solution
We can note down all possible sequences:

{H H H H}
{T H H H}
{H T H H}
{T T H H}
{H H T H}
{T H T H}
{H T T H}
{T T T H}
{H H H T}
{T H H T}
{H T H T}
{T T H T}
{H H T T}
{T H T T}
{H T T T}
{T T T T}

We see that there are 16 possible events. We find five events with three or more heads and so the probability is 5/16.

Note that the number of events is the number of ordered ways with repetition you can select four objects from two. The probability of getting three or more heads is the probability of getting either three heads exactly or four heads exactly. The number of events with three heads can be calculated as the number of ways in which you can place three heads into 4 spaces or $\binom{4}{3} = 4$. So the probability of exactly three heads in four flips is 4/16. Similarly for four heads in four flips we have $\binom{4}{4}/16 = 1/16$. So the total probability of three or more heads is 5/16.

Example 8.22

If two fair dice are thrown, what is the probability that they sum to five?

Solution
The total outcomes written as pairs are:

(1, 1), (1, 2), (1, 3), (1, 4), (1, 5), (1, 6).
(2, 1), (2, 2), (2, 3), (2, 4), (2, 5), (2, 6).
(3, 1), (3, 2), (3, 3), (3, 4), (3, 5), (3, 6).
(4, 1), (4, 2), (4, 3), (4, 4), (4, 5), (4, 6).
(5, 1), (5, 2), (5, 3), (5, 4), (5, 5), (5, 6).
(6, 1), (6, 2), (6, 3), (6, 4), (6, 5), (6, 6).

The total number of events is 36. Of those 36, there are four pairs that add to five (like (3, 2)) and so the probability of getting the sum five is 4/36 or 1/9. Note that the probability we were interested in calculating could be written as

P({(1, 4), (2, 3), (3, 2), (4, 1)}).

Bayes' rule

The outcomes for flipping two unbiased coins are:

H H
H T
T H
T T

The probability of getting two heads is 1/4. Suppose we are told that at least one coin landed on heads. What is the probability now that both coins landed on heads? The only outcomes that can now happen are

H H
H T
T H

So the probability of HH is 1/3.

If we are told that the first coin landed on heads the possible outcomes are

H H
H T

and so the probability of both heads is 1/2. This makes sense because now you are effectively only looking at the flip of one coin.

Figure 8.2 shows a Venn diagram for two events A and B. Event A is the first coin landing on heads and event B is the second coin landing on heads. Within the circle for A, there are two heads because two of the four outcomes have heads on the first coin; the same is true for the second coin. One head is written in the intersection of A and B, which represents the probability of two heads. If we want to calculate the probability of event A after being told that event B has happened (expressed as the 'probability of event A given B') our sample space is reduced to the objects enclosed by B. There are two Hs contained within B and one of these (the intersection) is also contained within A. So the probability of A given B is 1/2. For the coin problem, 'A given B' represents the probability of two heads given that the second coin landed on heads. We see that A given B is the ratio of the objects in the intersection of A and B to the number of objects in B. This ratio is known as the 'conditional probability'.

> The probability of event A given event B, called the 'conditional probability', denoted as $P(A \mid B)$ is
>
> $$P(A \mid B) = \frac{P(A \cap B)}{P(B)}$$

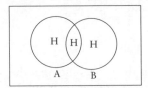

Figure 8.2   The possible outcomes for heads when two fair coins A and B are flipped.

Example 8.23

Three coins are flipped. What is the probability of three heads given that two heads have occurred?

Solution
To help us see the solution we shall write down all the possible outcomes.

H H H
T H H
H T H
T T H
H H T
T H T
H T T
T T T

If A is the event of three heads and B is the event of two heads we see that P(B) is 1/2 since four of the eight outcomes have two or more heads. The probability of both A and B (the intersection) is 1/8. So

$$P(A \mid B) = \frac{1/8}{1/2} = 1/4$$

We can confirm this answer by inspection because given B, the sample space is reduced to

H H H

T H H

H T H

H H T

of which one has three heads.

Instead of listing the outcomes we can use the principles of counting introduced earlier in the chapter. The number of outcomes is the number of ways in which three objects can be selected from a set of two with replacement (2^3). The number of strings of length three, with two heads is $\binom{3}{2}$, and three heads is $\binom{3}{3}$. The probability of two or more heads (P(B)) is $\dfrac{\binom{3}{2} + \binom{3}{3}}{2^3} = \dfrac{1}{2}$. The intersection of P(A) and P(B) is a string of length three with three heads and is $\dfrac{\binom{3}{3}}{2^3} = \dfrac{1}{8}$.

Example 8.24

If two fair dice are thrown, what is the probability that the second dice is greater than five given that the sum of both dice is greater than nine?

Solution
The total outcomes written as pairs are:

(1, 1), (1, 2), (1, 3), (1, 4), (1, 5), (1, 6).

(2, 1), (2, 2), (2, 3), (2, 4), (2, 5), (2, 6).

(3, 1), (3, 2), (3, 3), (3, 4), (3, 5), (3, 6).

(4, 1), (4, 2), (4, 3), (4, 4), (4, 5), (4, 6).

(5, 1), (5, 2), (5, 3), (5, 4), (5, 5), (5, 6).

(6, 1), (6, 2), (6, 3), (6, 4), (6, 5), (6, 6).

The pairs with a sum greater than nine are:

(4, 6).

(5, 5), (5, 6).

(6, 4), (6, 5), (6, 6).

Let A be the event that the second dice is greater than five and B be the event that the sum is greater than nine.

$$P(B) = 1/6 \quad P(A \cap B) = 3/36 = 1/12$$

$$P(A \mid B) = \frac{1/12}{1/6} = 1/2$$

> **Bayes' rule**
>
> Since we can write $P(A \mid B) = \dfrac{P(A \cap B)}{P(B)}$ and also $P(B \mid A) = \dfrac{P(A \cap B)}{P(A)}$
>
> with some rearrangement we get $P(B \mid A) = \dfrac{P(A \mid B)P(B)}{P(A)}$

One of the most useful properties of Bayes' rule is being able to relate $P(A \mid B)$ and $P(B \mid A)$. There are many situations in the real world in which we want $P(A \mid B)$ but it is not available but if we have $P(B \mid A)$ then we can find $P(A \mid B)$. Suppose we wish to find the probability that a patient has meningitis given that they have a stiff neck. If we have available the probability of a patient having a stiff neck given that they have meningitis, and the probability of a patient having meningitis, and the probability of a patient having a stiff neck, we can calculate the probability of meningitis given a stiff neck.

Independence

> Two events A and B are independent if $P(A \mid B) = P(A)$ which is the same as stating $P(A \cap B) = P(A) \cdot P(B)$

We would have little difficulty in accepting that drinking alcohol and driving a car increases the likelihood of an accident. Car accidents and the consumption of alcohol are dependent in a probabilistic sense. On the other hand you would not expect the colour of a driver's jacket to have any effect on the likelihood of the driver having an accident. The colour of the driver's jacket and having an accident are independent.

Example 8.25

If two fair dice are thrown, what is the probability that the second dice lands on three given that the first lands on two?

Solution
Let A be the event that the second dice lands on three and B be the event that the first dice lands on 2.

$$P(A) = 1/6 \quad P(A \cap B) = 1/36$$

$$P(A \mid B) = \frac{1/36}{1/6} = 1/6$$

We see that $P(A \mid B) = P(A)$ and so the two events are independent.

Example 8.26

What is the probability of the first dice landing on two and the second on three?

Solution
We know from Example 8.25 that these two events are independent. We wish to find $P(A \cap B)$. So we have $P(A) \cdot P(B) = 1/6 \cdot 1/6 = 1/36$.

Example 8.27

A tin contains five chocolate biscuits and ten plain. What is the probability of selecting a chocolate biscuit first followed by a plain biscuit assuming that the first biscuit is not put back in the tin?

Solution
There are 15 biscuits in total and so the chance of selecting a chocolate biscuit is 5/15 or 1/3. After selecting the chocolate biscuit there are now 14 left in the tin. The chance of selecting a plain biscuit on the second selection is 10/14. Both selections are independent and so the probability of selecting a chocolate biscuit first followed by a plain biscuit is $1/3 \cdot 10/14 = 5/21$.

Example 8.28

A tin contains five chocolate biscuits and ten plain. What is the probability of selecting a chocolate biscuit and a plain biscuit assuming that the first biscuit is not put back in the tin?

Solution
We are not concerned with order here. First we shall find the number of ways in which two biscuits can be selected. We have an unorderd selection without repetition because the same biscuit cannot be selected twice. So the number of ways in which we can select two biscuits is $\binom{15}{2}$. Now we need to know in how many ways we can combine a chocolate biscuit with a plain biscuit; to answer this we use the multiplication principle. If we let c denote a chocolate biscuit and p a plain biscuit and if we number them we have:

$$c_1 c_2 c_3 c_4 c_5 p_1 p_2 p_3 p_4 p_5 p_6 p_7 p_8 p_9 p_{10}$$

We can select the first chocolate biscuit with any of the plain biscuits to give ten combinations and we can repeat this five times for each chocolate biscuit to give 50 combinations of a chocolate biscuit with a plain biscuit. So the probability of selecting a chocolate biscuit and a plain biscuit is

$$\frac{50}{\binom{15}{2}} = 10/21$$

8.3

Answers appear in Appendix A.

1 Given $P(B) = 0.4$ and $P(A \cap B) = 0.2$ find $P(A|B)$.

2 Using the result from Question 1 and given that $P(B|A) = 0.4$ find $P(A)$.

3 Given $P(A) = 0.3$ and $P(B) = 0.2$ and that $P(A)$ and $P(B)$ are independent find $P(A \cap B)$.

4 What is the probability of throwing two fair dice and the first landing on a three and the second landing on the number four or higher?

5 If two fair dice are thrown, what is the probability that the second dice is greater than or equal to three given that the sum of both dice is greater than eight?

6 There are three balls in a bag numbered 1, 2 and 3. If a ball is selected without replacement, what is the probability of selecting the balls in order (i.e., ball 1 first, ball 2 second and ball 3 third)?

7 There are three balls in a bag numbered 1, 2 and 3. If two balls are selected without replacement, what is the probability of selecting ball 1 and ball 2?

Fuzzy systems

When we studied logic and set theory we took the view that things are black or white: a statement is true or it is false, a conclusion can or cannot be proved from the assumptions, an object either belongs or does not belong to a set, a set is or is not a subset, etc. Fuzzy systems are based upon the belief that the world is grey and better modelled as being grey. For example, a rule of the road for car drivers is:

> If the road is wet Then allow more time to brake

How do we define wet? Is it when the road is flooded? Is it when the road is slightly damp? Is it when the road is very damp? How do we define more time?

In everyday language we use symbols that have fuzzy boundaries. The word tall is a fuzzy symbol. Is Dave, who is six feet in height, tall? Dave might be considered tall by Simon who is five foot ten but Dave might not be tall in the eyes of Jamie who is six foot four. Suppose we desire to create a set of tall people from a team of rugby players. We could follow traditional set theory and define the property of membership as a discrete function; the property that every member of the set share is that they are all over six foot tall. If you are one of the rugby players you are either a member or not; membership maps to 1 or 0, so member(Peter) maps to 0 because Peter is less than six foot but member(John) maps to 1 because John is over six foot. We are attempting to see which of the rugby players is associated with the concept of being tall and our definition for the set tall fails. Why does it fail? Ask an audience to class the players as tall or not tall. If a player is seven foot tall no doubt there would be wide agreement amongst the audience that this player is tall and everyone in the audience would answer with complete confidence. Show the player who is five foot eleven and doubt creeps in. Ask a member of the audience for their opinion and the response might be – the player is tall but not that tall.

Some symbols or questions in the world appear to be black and white. For instance, the definition in law for the symbol married is black and white: either someone is or is not a member of the set of married people. Ask someone though who is separated from a partner and going through divorce if they are married and see if you get a yes or no reply.

A fuzzy system represents knowledge as fuzzy rules and these rules are used to perform fuzzy reasoning. A traditional symbol system would use many rules to represent the rule:

If the room temperature is low Then turn up the heater

Instead of using the fuzzy term 'low' and the fuzzy term 'turn up' you could use discrete values like 0 °C, 12 °C, 15 °C … to create many rules. A fuzzy system allows you to express the knowledge symbolically as

If the room temperature is low Then turn up the heater

but with the advantage that this rule does the job of tens, maybe hundreds, maybe thousands of discrete rules.

Fuzzy theory is underpinned with mathematics. Fuzzy theory uses the terminology of set theory, relations and logic. There are for example definitions for a fuzzy set, the intersection of two fuzzy sets, the union of two fuzzy sets, the complement of a fuzzy set, etc.

In Chapter 2 we defined the universal set as the set of all objects that we are interested in for an application. So for the set of tall people our universal set was the players of a rugby team. In traditional set theory, there is a membership function for a set that maps every object in the universal set to the value 1 if the object is a member of the set and to the value 0 if the object is not a member. In fuzzy logic it is usual to use the term 'universe of discourse' to refer to the universal set. With fuzzy sets an object can belong to some degree; an object's membership does not have to map to either being in or out of the set.

> A fuzzy membership function maps every object x from the universe of discourse X to a number between 0 and 1. The membership function for a set A is denoted by $\mu_A(x)$ and for an object x it returns a number between 0 and 1; this number gives the degree of membership. We express this more formally as
>
> $$\mu_A(x) : X \rightarrow [0,1]$$

In traditional set theory we can define a set by listing all of its members. We can do the same with fuzzy sets but each member is written as an ordered pair where the first argument denotes the object and the second argument gives the object's degree of membership.

A fuzzy set defined on X can be written as a collection of ordered pairs

$$A = \{(x, \mu_A(x))\}, x \in X$$

Example 8.29

Given the membership function for the variable (symbol) tall as that in Figure 8.3, list the set of tall people for the people listed below:

Dave   172 0.04
Peter   178 0.25
John   180 0.47
Roy   190 0.98
Gavin   195 0.99

Solution
The degree of membership can be read from the curve.

   {(Dave, 0.04), (Peter, 0.25), (John, 0.47), (Roy, 0.98), (Gavin, 0.99)}

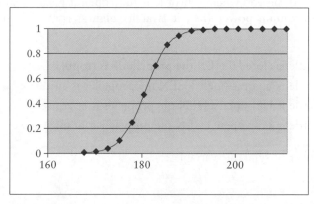

Figure 8.3   A membership function for the variable Tall. The degree of membership for a height in centimetres can be read from the curve.

The union of two fuzzy sets A and B is another fuzzy set with membership function

$$\mu_{A \cup B}(x) = \max(\mu_A(x), \mu_B(x))$$

This definition says that the degree of membership of $A \cup B$ is the maximum of the two values $\mu_A(x)$ and $\mu_B(x)$. The union of two fuzzy sets is related to the fuzzy logic OR.

The intersection of two fuzzy sets A and B is another fuzzy set with membership function

$$\mu_{A \cap B}(x) = \min(\mu_A(x),\ \mu_B(x))$$

This definition says that the degree of membership of $A \cap B$ is the minimum of the two values $\mu_A(x)$ and $\mu_B(x)$. The intersection of two fuzzy sets is related to the fuzzy logic AND.

There are three steps to building a fuzzy system.

1. Decide on the symbols or fuzzy variables.
2. Select sets for those fuzzy variables.
3. Select the fuzzy rules of the form IF x THEN y.

An example should help make clear each one of these steps. We shall consider a rule that relates the throttle setting of a piston engine aircraft to the revolutions per minute (rpm) of the propeller. The throttle of an aircraft determines how fast the propeller turns. Many small aircraft have a push-pull throttle which is basically a horizontal rod that slides in and out. When a throttle is closed it means that the propeller is not turning and when a throttle is fully open it means that the engine is generating its maximum power (i.e., it is at its highest rpm). The rules for our example are:

> IF the throttle is closed THEN the propeller has stopped
>
> IF the throttle is quarter-open THEN the propeller is at idle
>
> IF the throttle is half-open THEN the propeller is at cruise
>
> IF the throttle is fully open THEN the propeller is at max-power

There are a number of symbolic variables:

> Closed
>
> Quarter-open
>
> Half-open
>
> Fully-open
>
> Stopped
>
> Idle
>
> Cruise
>
> Max-power

We need to select the fuzzy sets for these symbolic variables but before that can be done we need a way of measuring the position of the throttle. The throttle position can be measured as indicated in Figure 8.4.

cm

Fully open   Closed

Figure 8.4   Throttle positions shown fully open and closed.

The fuzzy sets have been defined in Figures 8.5 and 8.6.

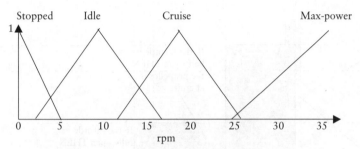

Figure 8.5   Fuzzy membership functions for rpm variables.

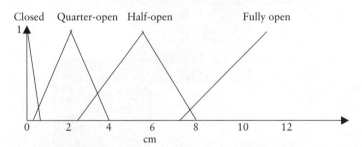

Figure 8.6   Fuzzy membership functions for throttle position variables.

The fuzzy sets in this case have membership functions that are triangular regions. The graphs depict the degree of membership to the symbolic variables. For example, the degree of membership, for the value 5 cm (throttle position), to the set half-open can be read from the graph.

Through the fuzzy sets the rules are associated with numbers. Each rule is the mathematical product of two triangles. For example, the rule

IF the throttle is half-open THEN the propeller is at cruise

is the mathematical product of the half-open triangle with the cruise triangle. A mathematical product describes a region. For example, the product of two lines is a rectangle and the product of a disk and a circle is doughnut shaped. The product of the two triangles is a complicated 3D shape that looks a little like a four-sided tent. The base of the tent (the floor) is a 2D region which contains the pair of numbers (throttle position, rpm) and the height of this tent represents the degree to which a point belongs to the rule. These regions (products) are called 'patches'. The idea of patches is illustrated in Figure 8.7 but these patches are just 2D squares and are therefore a highly simplified representation of the real shape.

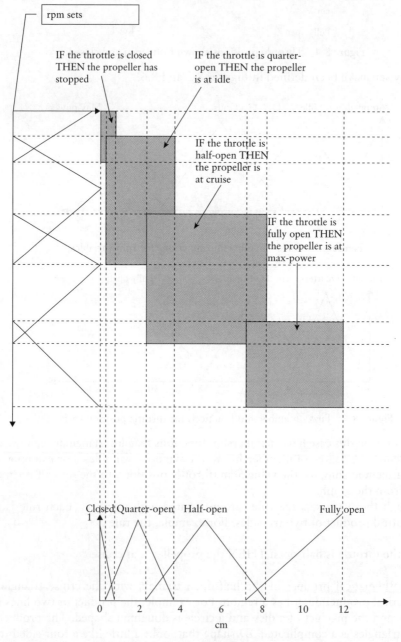

Figure 8.7   Rule patches (the idea for presenting this diagram is borrowed from Bart Kosko's book *Fuzzy Thinking*, 1994).

The rules are of the form

IF x THEN y

Each rule relates a value of a symbolic variable (like throttle position) to a value of another symbolic variable (like rpm). The rules can be seen as a symbolic description of a function as shown in Figure 8.8.

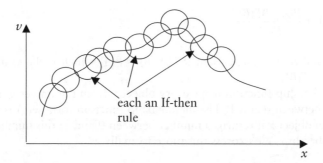

Figure 8.8   Using rules symbolically to describe $y = f(x)$.

Summary

- **Addition principle**
  If k disjoint subsets can be formed from a set of objects with n_i objects in subset i then we get $n_1 + n_2 + \ldots + n_k$ objects all together.
- **Multiplication principle**
  If the are n_i possible outcomes for event i, and there are k events, then there are $n_1 \times n_2 \times \ldots \times n_k$ possible outcomes for the sequence of events.
  For the selection of k objects from a set of n objects:

	Ordered	Unordered
Repetition	n^k	$\dbinom{n + k - 1}{k}$
No repetition	$P(n,k) = \dfrac{n!}{(n - k)!}$	$\dfrac{n!}{k!(n - k)!}$ denoted by $\dbinom{n}{k}$

The binomial theorem for real values a and b, and positive integer n states:

$$(a + b)^n = \binom{n}{0}a^n b^0 + \binom{n}{1}a^{n-1}b^1 + \binom{n}{2}a^{n-2}b^2 + \ldots + \binom{n}{n}a^0 b^n$$

- **Properties of probability**
  (a) The sum of all event probabilities drawn from a sample space add to 1
  (b) $P(E^c) = 1 - P(E)$ For event E
  (c) $P(E_1 \cup E_2) = P(E_1) + P(E_2) - P(E_1 \cap E_2)$ for events E_1 and E_2. This is the probability of event E_1 or E_2. Either E_1 occurs or E_2 occurs or both.

The probability of event A given event B, called the conditional probability, denoted as $P(A \mid B)$ is

$$P(A \mid B) = \frac{P(A \cap B)}{P(B)}$$

- **Bayes' rule**

$$P(B \mid A) = \frac{P(A \mid B)P(B)}{P(A)}$$

Two events A and B are independent if $P(A \mid B) = P(A)$ which is the same as stating $P(A \cap B) = P(A) \cdot P(B)$.

A fuzzy membership function maps every object x from the universe of discourse X to a number between 0 and 1. The membership function for a set A is denoted by $\mu_A(x)$ and for an object x it returns a number between 0 and 1; this number gives the degree of membership. We express this more formally as

$$\mu_A(x) : X \rightarrow [0,1]$$

A fuzzy set defined on X can be written as a collection of ordered pairs

$$A = \{(x, \mu_A(x))\}, x \in X$$

There are three steps to building a fuzzy system:

1. Decide on the symbols or fuzzy variables.

2. Select sets for those fuzzy variables.

3. Select the fuzzy rules of the form IF x THEN y.

Applications

Bayes' rule allows unknown probabilities to be computed from known probabilities and this rule is the basis for building probabilistic reasoning systems. Probabilistic reasoning forms part of artificial intelligence which is the study of trying to put human-like intelligence into machines. Probabilistic reasoning attempts to keep a system's behaviour to an acceptable level when presented with uncertain information. In the real world we operate all the time with uncertainty. You can never leave home for college or work and be certain that you will arrive on time. You can estimate from measurement the likelihood that you will arrive on time. During the process of diagnosing a patient, a doctor is rarely certain of what a patient is suffering from. The doctor makes observations and takes measurements to increase the confidence of a diagnosis.

Fuzzy sets and fuzzy logic are also used in intelligent systems. Fuzzy systems have had a high degree of commercial success in control applications. Fuzzy logic has been used in camcorders, gearboxes, electric shavers and many other commercial goods.

Probabilistic systems deal with uncertainty whereas fuzzy systems deal with vagueness; there is a difference. If you wish to create a basketball team from next year's intake of undergraduates you will be uncertain about how many will be over six feet tall. You can use probability to give a measure of uncertainty because measures exist for the height of a population. Once your new undergraduates arrive you can find out with certainty which players are over six feet. If someone says to you that they want a basketball team made up of tall undergraduates and they leave you to select the team there is an element of vagueness about whether your selection of players satisfy being tall.

There are a number of debates that sometimes carry on for years within computing science and one fierce debate has concerned fuzzy systems. Supporters of fuzzy systems believe that fuzzy logic and fuzzy set theory is the basis for significant breakthroughs for developing intelligent systems. Opponents will argue that whilst there is a large degree of commercial success with fuzzy systems, the commercial products rely on small rule sets and the limitation of fuzzy systems will be revealed when the rule bases are scaled up. The debate is of interest to those who are involved in developing new techniques for building intelligent systems so that an assessment can be made about which research avenues might be more prosperous. If you are building systems for today you can be pragmatic and select the best approach for the application. One comforting thought is that all the approaches require the same mathematical skill set and it is wise to be aware of emerging technology.

Neural networks are computing devices that are also used in building intelligent systems. We mentioned neural networks at the end of Chapter 6. Neural networks are parallel computing machines that use many simple processors that communicate through weighted connections. One of their main attractions is that they can learn a task rather than being programmed in a conventional way. A neural network can be represented as a weighted graph with the processors seen as nodes and the connections as edges with weight values. The graph is normally directed because signals usually travel in one direction. A neural network learns by adapting the weighted values and a learning algorithm controls the way in which these weights adapt. These algorithms are flexible, for instance, the same algorithm can be applied to a task that involves image recognition or a task that involves image compression. One drawback with neural networks is that they can be slow to learn. Fuzzy logic has been successfully applied to speed up learning. Another type of neural network is based upon probability theory. A network known as a probabilistic neural network learns almost instantaneously. The probabilistic neural network is really a Bayesian classifier; a Bayesian classifier uses Bayes' rule to classify patterns. Many tasks can be seen as a task of classification, for example, an aircraft can be classed as friend or foe.

EXERCISES

Answers appear in Appendix B.

1 A restaurant menu has six starters, ten main courses and six desserts. How many items are on the menu?

2 A bicycle shop can provide a choice of eight models. For each model a customer has a choice of four colours and three sizes. How many options are there in total?

3 How many strings of length six can be constructed from the characters {0, 1}?

4 In how many ways can the characters WH564 be arranged?

5 How many strings can be made of length three from the set of characters {A, B, C, D, E, F}?

6 How many strings can be made of length three from the set of characters {A, B, C, D, E, G} if repeated characters are not allowed?

7 A business has advertised two software engineering posts and 15 people have been selected for interview. How many selections can be made?

8 A business has 12 software engineers from which it wishes to appoint a senior software engineer and a project manager. How many options are available for the company to choose from?

9 A project team of four is to be selected from nine people. How many possible selections are there?

10 A graph contains a series of vertices arranged in layers. In the first layer there are three vertices and they all connect to four vertices in the next layer which in turn connect to six vertices in a final layer. Assuming that the connections are directed, how many connections are there in total?

11 How many strings of length three or less can be generated from the characters {A, B, C}?

12 There are six coloured counters: four blue and two red. In how many ways can these counters be arranged in a line?

13 A bag contains the names of six horses to run in a race. You select a name from the bag. What is the probability of picking the winner?

14 Two cricket teams, A and B, are to play a series of five matches. A coin is flipped at the start of each match to see which team has the option of batting. What is the probability of team A having the option for all five matches?

15 Two dice are thrown. What is the probability of the total score being greater than six?

16 There are eight horses due to run in a race. You make a bet on the first, second and third to finish. Assuming all horses have an equal chance of winning what is the probability that you win the bet?

17 A network administrator issues five-digit identity (digits 0 to 9) numbers to its users. What is the chance of someone gaining illegal access to the network?

18 Given $P(B) = 0.6$ and $P(A \cap B) = 0.4$ find $P(A \mid B)$.

19 Three coins are flipped. What is the probability of all three coins showing tails given that at least one coin is showing tails.

20 Two dice are thrown. What is the probability of both dice showing a four given that at least one is showing a four?

9

Proof by induction

Introduction

Mathematics often expresses results in the form $P \rightarrow Q$. We have seen some examples of how to prove expressions of the form $P \rightarrow Q$ in Chapter 1; we write a series of statements with each statement being either an assumption or the result of applying a rule of inference. There are a number of general proof techniques but one that is frequently applicable is known as 'proof by induction'.

Proof by induction

Examine the following snippet of C++ code:

```
int n = 1;
int m = 10;
if(pow(2, 1) > 1){
   while( n < m){
      if(pow(2, n) > n)
         n = n + 1;
   }
}
cout << n << endl;
```

This program is the following:

$n \in N$	(n is a positive integer)
$m \in N$	(m is a positive integer)
$n: = 1$	(set $n = 1$)
$m: = 10$	(set $m = 10$)
if$(2^n > n)$	(statement must be true to do the next three lines)
while $(n < m)$	(the if statement will be tested while n is less than m)
if$(2^n > n)$	
$n: = n + 1$	
print n	

The program will print out 10. This short piece of code checks that

$2^n > n$ holds for positive integers 0 to 9

If we want to check it holds for integers 0 to 1000 then the loop has to execute many more times. Suppose we want to check it for any positive integer? Mathematical induction gives us a way of proving that $2^n > n$ holds for any positive integer. Mathematical induction says that if you can prove $2^n > n$ for $n = 1$ and you can prove it for $n + 1$ then it is proved for any positive integer value of n. So there is no need for the loop, only two steps are involved.

> To prove a proposition $P(n)$ for any positive integer, we need to perform two steps:
>
> 1. $P(1)$ The property is true for 1.
> 2. For all positive integers, if $P(n)$ is true then $P(n + 1)$ is true.

Step 1 is called the 'basis for the induction' and step 2 is called the 'inductive step'. Induction says that if you show both of these steps to be true, then the proposition is true for all positive integers.

Example 9.1

Show that

$$1 + 2 + 3 + \dots + n = \frac{1}{2}n(n + 1)$$

This is the sum of the integers 1 to n. The right-hand side states that instead of using a loop to sum integers we can find the sum using

$$\frac{1}{2}n(n + 1)$$

For example, if $n = 5$ we have

$$1 + 2 + 3 + 4 + 5 = \frac{1}{2}5(5 + 1) = 15$$

Solution
Step 1 we check $P(1)$ which is

$$1 = \frac{1}{2}1(1 + 1) \quad \text{substitute 1 into the formula}$$

Step 1 is clearly true.

For step 2 we check for $k + 1$. The left-hand side of the expression says that we add $k + 1$ to the sum. For the right-hand side we substitute $k + 1$ for n.

$$1 + 2 + 3 + \ldots + k + k + 1 = \frac{1}{2}(k + 1)((k + 1) + 1) \quad \text{this is for } P(k + 1)$$

In case you are not happy with this, let us check with a value of $k = 3$. The expression above is for $P(k + 1)$ but we want to check $P(k)$ which is

$$1 + 2 + 3 + \ldots + k = \frac{1}{2}k(k + 1)$$

So $P(3)$ is 6. Now, to check $P(k + 1)$ we substitute 4 into $P(k)$ to give 10. The same result can be found by putting 3 into

$$1 + 2 + 3 + \ldots + k + k + 1 = \frac{1}{2}(k + 1)((k + 1) + 1)$$

to give

$$1 + 2 + 3 + 4 = \frac{1}{2}(3 + 1)((3 + 1) + 1)$$

Assuming we are happy with the meaning of these expressions we now need to show that

$$1 + 2 + 3 + \ldots + k + k + 1 = \frac{1}{2}(k + 1)((k + 1) + 1)$$

If we assume that the proposition is true then

$$\frac{1}{2}k(k + 1) + k + 1 = \frac{1}{2}(k + 1)((k + 1) + 1)$$

$$= \frac{1}{2}(k + 1)(k + 2)$$

$$= \frac{1}{2}(k^2 + 3k + 2)$$

$$= \frac{1}{2}(k(k + 1) + 2(k + 1))$$

$$= \frac{1}{2}k(k + 1) + (k + 1)$$

The last step shows that the right-hand side is the same as the left-hand side and so the second step is proved and together with step 1 shows that the proposition holds for any positive integer.

Example 9.2

Prove by induction that

$$1^3 + 2^3 + 3^3 + \ldots + n^3 = \frac{n^2(n + 1)^2}{4}$$

Solution
Step 1

$$1 = \frac{1^2(1+1)^2}{4}$$

Step 2

$$1^3 + 2^3 + 3^3 + \dots + k^3 + (k+1)^3 = \frac{(k+1)^2\,(k+1+1)^2}{4}$$

$$\frac{k^2(k+1)^2}{4} + (k+1)^3 = \frac{(k+1)^2\,(k+1+1)^2}{4}$$

$$= \frac{(k+1)^2\,(k+2)(k+2)}{4}$$

$$= \frac{(k+1)^2\,(k^2+4k+4)}{4}$$

$$= \frac{(k+1)^2 k^2 + 4(k+1)^2\,(k+1)}{4}$$

$$= \frac{k^2(k+1)^2}{4} + (k+1)^3$$

Example 9.3

Prove by induction that

$$2^n > n$$

Solution
Step 1

$$2^1 > 1$$

Step 2
(a) $2^{k+1} > k+1$
(b) $= 2 \cdot 2^k > k+1$
(c) $2 \cdot 2^k > 2k$ \qquad since we assume $2^k > k$
(d) $2k \geq k+1$ \qquad equal for $k = 1$
(e) $2 \cdot 2^k > k+1$

Note that (b) says the same as (a). For (c) we have assumed that the proposition is true and so if both sides are multiplied by 2 the proposition will still be true.

? **9.1**

Answer appears in Appendix A.

1 Prove by induction that $1 + 3 + \ldots + (2n + 1) = (n + 1)^2$. Note that for $n = 1$ the left-hand side is $1 + 3$.

Summary

> To prove a proposition $P(n)$ for any positive integer, we need to perform two steps:
>
> 1. $P(1)$ The property is true for 1.
> 2. For all positive integers, if $P(n)$ is true then $P(n + 1)$ is true.

EXERCISES

Answers are not given for these exercises.

1 Prove that $2 + 4 + 6 + \ldots + 2n = n(n + 1)$

2 Prove that $1 + 4 + 9 + \ldots + n^2 = \dfrac{n(n + 1)(2n + 1)}{6}$

Appendix A

Answers to in-text questions

1.1

1 (a) T (b) T (c) T (d) T (e) T (f) T (g) F (h) T

2 Translate the following logical expressions into English

  A – today is Thursday   B – tomorrow is Friday

(a) Today is Thursday and tomorrow is Friday
(b) Either today is Thursday or tomorrow is Friday
(c) If today is Thursday then tomorrow is Friday

3

A	B	$A \wedge B$	$\neg(A \wedge B)$	$\neg A \vee \neg B$
T	T	T	F	F
F	T	F	T	T
T	F	F	T	T
F	F	F	T	T

We see that the last two columns are the same and so $\neg(A \wedge B)$ is equivalent to $\neg A \vee \neg B$. Note that in the last column, the $\neg$ is applied before $\vee$.

4

A	B	C	$A \wedge B$	$(A \wedge B) \wedge C$	$B \wedge C$	$A \wedge (B \wedge C)$
T	T	T	T	T	T	T
F	T	T	F	F	T	F
T	F	T	F	F	F	F
F	F	T	F	F	F	F
T	T	F	T	F	F	F
F	T	F	F	F	F	F
T	F	F	F	F	F	F
F	F	F	F	F	F	F

5 Since P is T and Q is F the definition for OR gives $P \vee Q$ a value of T. Since the left-hand side of $\rightarrow$ is T and the right-hand side is T then $(P \vee Q) \rightarrow P$ is T.

1.2

1 (a) $B \wedge C$
   (b) $B \vee C$
   (c) $B \rightarrow C$
   (d) $A \rightarrow B$

2 (a) Contradiction
   (b) Tautology
   (c)

1 A	2 B	3 C	4 $A \wedge B$	5 $(A \wedge B) \wedge C$	6 $B \wedge C$	7 $A \wedge (B \wedge C)$	8 $5 \leftrightarrow 7$
T	T	T	T	T	T	T	T
F	T	T	F	F	T	F	T
T	F	T	F	F	F	F	T
F	F	T	F	F	F	F	T
T	T	F	T	F	F	F	T
F	T	F	F	F	F	F	T
T	F	F	F	F	F	F	T
F	F	F	F	F	F	F	T

Column 8 is the equivalence connective applied to columns 5 and 7. Column 8 shows that the expression is a Tautology.

1.3

1 (a)

P	Q	$P \rightarrow Q$	$Q \vee P$	$(P \rightarrow Q) \wedge (Q \vee P)$	$(P \rightarrow Q) \wedge (Q \vee P) \rightarrow Q$
T	T	T	T	T	T
F	T	T	T	T	T
T	F	F	T	F	T
F	F	T	F	F	T

The last column shows that the argument is valid.

   (b)

1 P	2 Q	3 R	4 $P \wedge Q$	5 $(P \wedge Q) \rightarrow R$	6 $4 \wedge 5$	7 $6 \rightarrow R$
T	T	T	T	T	T	T
F	T	T	F	T	F	T
T	F	T	F	T	F	T
F	F	T	F	T	F	T
T	T	F	T	F	F	T
F	T	F	F	T	F	T
T	F	F	F	T	F	T
F	F	F	F	T	F	T

Column 6 is the AND of columns 4 and 5. Column 7 is the implication of column 6 with column 3 (R). Column 7 shows that the argument is valid.

2 (a) 1. $P \rightarrow Q$ assumption
        2. $Q \vee P$ assumption
        3. $Q \rightarrow Q$ tautology used simply to make the last step obvious
        4. Q $\vee$ elimination on 1, 2, 3

   (b) 1. P assumption
        2. Q assumption
        3. $P \wedge Q$ $\wedge$ introduction on 1 and 2
        4. $(P \wedge Q) \rightarrow R$ assumption
        5. R from 3 and 4 with modus-ponens

2.1

1 (a) True   (b) False   (c) True   (d) False

2 (a) $\{5, 6, 7\}$
   (b) $\{5, 6, 8\}$
   (c) $\{-8, -1, 0, 1, 8\}$

2.2

1 (a) False   (b) False   (c) True   (d) True

2 (a) False   (b) True   (c) True

2.3

1 (a) {Carl, John, David, Sara, Debbie}
   (b) {David}
   (c) {Carl, John}
   (d) {Sheila, Janet}
   (e) 3
   (f) {{}, {Carl}, {John}, {David}, {Carl, John}, {Carl, David}, {John, David}, {Carl, John, David}}

3.1

1 (a) likes(John, fish)
   (b) likes(John, fish) $\wedge$ likes(John, chips)
   (c) own(Sara, dog) $\vee$ own(Sara, horse)
   (d) $\forall x.[\text{dog}(x) \rightarrow \text{like}(x, \text{bone})]$
   (e) $\exists x.[\text{dog}(x) \wedge \text{like}(x, \text{bone})]$
   (f) $\forall x.[\text{dog}(x) \wedge \text{own}(\text{Sue}, x)) \rightarrow \text{small}(x)]$
   (g) $\forall x. \exists y.[\text{loves}(x, y)]$
   (h) $\exists y. \forall x.[\text{loves}(x, y)]$

4.1

1 (a) {(2, 3), (3, 2)}   (b) {(1, 2), (1, 3), (2, 1), (2, 2), (2, 3), (3, 1), (3, 2), (3, 3)}

2 (a) True   (b) True
(c) False – Brian is not in the set and cannot appear in the set of ordered pairs.

4.2

1 (a) symmetric   (b) transitive   (c) transitive   (d) reflexive, symmetric, transitive
(e) reflexive, symmetric, transitive.

4.3

1 (a) function   (b) Not a function – a appears twice   (c) function
(d) No because 4 is not a member of the codomain   (e) function

2 (a) one–one, onto, bijective   (b) not one–one: two inputs give same output; not
onto: range does not equal codomain   (c) one–one, onto, bijective
(d) one–one, onto, bijective.

4.4

1 (a) 8   (b) 1   (c) −2   (d) −9

2 {(brain, nia), (transport, tro), (park, kra)}

5.1

1 (a) $[-3 \quad 5 \quad 6]$
(b) $[-9 \quad 3 \quad 0]$
(c) $[-12 \quad 8 \quad 6]$
(d) $\sqrt{61}$
(e) -5
(f) $\begin{bmatrix} 3 \\ 1 \\ 3 \end{bmatrix}$

2 (a) $[10 \quad -5 \quad 0 \quad 3]$
(b) $[-2 \quad 1 \quad 2 \quad -1]$
(c) $[8 \quad -4 \quad 2 \quad 2]$
(d) $\sqrt{22}$
(e) 31
$\begin{bmatrix} 6 \\ -3 \\ -1 \\ 2 \end{bmatrix}$

5.2

1 (a) 2

(b) $\begin{bmatrix} 8 & 12 & 10 \\ 2 & -6 & 4 \end{bmatrix}$

(c) $\begin{bmatrix} 3 & 26 & 62 \\ 18 & -1 & 2 \end{bmatrix}$

(d) $\begin{bmatrix} -1 & -3 & 5 \\ 1 & 2 & 2 \\ 2 & 4 & 6 \end{bmatrix}$

(e) $\begin{bmatrix} 77 & -4 \\ -4 & 14 \end{bmatrix}$

5.3

$\begin{bmatrix} 3 & 1 & -1 & | & 2 \\ 0 & 1\frac{2}{3} & 1\frac{1}{3} & | & 7\frac{1}{3} \\ 0 & 1\frac{2}{3} & 3\frac{1}{3} & | & 3\frac{1}{3} \end{bmatrix}$ $\begin{array}{l} R_2 = R_2 - R_1/3 \\ R_3 = R_3 - R_1/3 \end{array}$

$\begin{bmatrix} 3 & 1 & -1 & | & 2 \\ 0 & 5 & 4 & | & 22 \\ 0 & 5 & 10 & | & 10 \end{bmatrix}$ $\begin{array}{l} R_2 = 3R_2 \\ R_3 = 3R_3 \end{array}$

$\begin{bmatrix} 3 & 1 & -1 & | & 2 \\ 0 & 5 & 4 & | & 22 \\ 0 & 0 & 6 & | & -12 \end{bmatrix}$ $R_3 = R_3 - R_2$

$x_3 = -2$

$5x_2 + 4 \times -2 = 22$

$x_2 = 6$

$3x_1 + 6 + 2 = 2$

$x_1 = -2$

6.1

1 $(2 \times 3) - (1 \times -2) = 8$

$(1 \times 1) - (3 \times 2) = -5$

2 Minors are:

$\begin{vmatrix} 2 & -1 \\ 1 & 2 \end{vmatrix} \begin{vmatrix} 2 & 1 \\ 1 & 2 \end{vmatrix} \begin{vmatrix} 2 & 1 \\ 2 & -1 \end{vmatrix}$

$-4 \begin{vmatrix} 2 & -1 \\ 1 & 2 \end{vmatrix} + 0 \begin{vmatrix} 2 & 1 \\ 1 & 2 \end{vmatrix} + 0 \begin{vmatrix} 2 & 1 \\ 2 & -1 \end{vmatrix} = -20$

3 $A^T = \begin{bmatrix} 2 & 2 & 1 \\ 4 & 0 & 0 \\ 1 & -1 & 2 \end{bmatrix}$ $adjA = \begin{bmatrix} 0 & -8 & -4 \\ -5 & 3 & 4 \\ 0 & 4 & -8 \end{bmatrix}$

$A^{-1} = -\dfrac{1}{20} \begin{bmatrix} 0 & -8 & -4 \\ -5 & 3 & 4 \\ 0 & 4 & -8 \end{bmatrix}$

7.1

1 (a) Yes

(b) Node1 degree 4, Node2 degree 2, Node3 degree 4, Node4 degree 4

(c) $\begin{bmatrix} 1 & 0 & 1 & 1 \\ 0 & 0 & 1 & 1 \\ 1 & 1 & 0 & 2 \\ 1 & 1 & 2 & 0 \end{bmatrix}$

(d) Example solution to include vertices in the order 3-1-4-2-3

(e) $\begin{bmatrix} 3 & 2 & 3 & 3 \\ 2 & 2 & 2 & 2 \\ 3 & 2 & 6 & 2 \\ 3 & 2 & 2 & 6 \end{bmatrix}$

7.2

1 A solution

V = [2]
E = [e2] V = [2, 4]
E = [e2, e5] V = [2, 4, 3]
E = [e2, e5, e4] V = [2, 4, 3, 1]
E = [e2, e5, e4, e1] V = [2, 4, 3, 1, 1]
E = [e2, e5, e4, e1, e6] V = [2, 4, 3, 1, 1, 4]
E = [e2, e5, e4, e1, e6, e7] V = [2, 4, 3, 1, 1, 4, 3]
E = [e2, e5, e4, e1, e6, e7, e3] V = [2, 4, 3, 1, 1, 4, 3, 2]

7.3

1

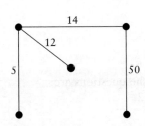

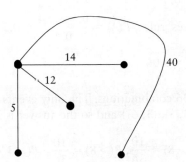

2 W = [5, 12, 14, 15, 18, 32, 40, 50, 70] edges are built as follows
   E = [5]
   E = [5, 12]
   E = [5, 12, 14]
   E = [5, 12, 14, 15]

3 Preorder: a b d h i j k e c f g
   Postorder: h j k i d e b f g c a

8.1

1 (a) 24   (b) 40320

2 (a) 120   (b) 132   (c) 5040   (d) 6   (e) 6

3 (a) 593775   (b) 45   (c) 1

4 (a) Ordered without repetition 5040

   (b) Unordered without repetition 210

5 P(10, 10)

6 Unordered without repetition 1365

7 Ordered without repetition 380

8 Assume an ordered selection and no repetition 132

8.2

1 $(1 + x)^5 = \binom{5}{0}1^5x^0 + \binom{5}{1}1^4x^1 + \binom{5}{2}1^3x^2 + \binom{5}{3}1^2x^3 + \binom{5}{4}1^1x^4 + \binom{5}{5}1^0x^5$

   and so the coefficient for x^3 is 10 and for x^5 is 1.

2 This corresponds to the binomial expansion for $(1 + 1)^2 = 4$.

8.3

1 $P(A \mid B) = \dfrac{0.2}{0.4} = 0.5$

2 Using Bayes' rule $P(A) = \dfrac{0.5 \times 0.4}{0.4} = 0.5$

3 $0.3 \times 0.2 = 0.06$

4 Total of 36 combinations. The only events satisfying the questions are:
   $\{(3, 4), (3, 5), (3, 6)\}$ and so the answer is $3/36 = 1/12$.

5 $P(\geq 3 \cap > 8) = \dfrac{10}{36}, P(> 8) = \dfrac{10}{36}$ $P(\geq 3 \mid > 8) = 1$

6 Number of ordered selections without repetition is P(3, 3) = 6. We want one of these selections and so the probability is 1/6.

7 Selections are P(3, 2). Two of the selections will satisfy the solution and so the answer is 1/3. Alternatively, we want one from an unordered selection of two items from three.

9.1

Step 1 $1 + 3 = (1 + 1)^2$ is true

Step 2 $1 + 3 + \ldots + (2k + 1) + (2(k + 1) + 1) = ((k + 1) + 1)^2$

$$(k + 1)^2 + (2(k + 1) + 1) = ((k + 1) + 1)^2$$
$$= ((k + 1) + 1)((k + 1) + 1)$$
$$= (k + 1)^2 + (2(k + 1) + 1)$$

Appendix B

Answers to exercises

Chapter 1

1 (a) Yes   (b) No   (c) Yes   (d) No

2 (a) T   (b) F   (c) F   (d) T   (e) F   (f) T   (g) T   (h) T

3 (a)

P	Q	$P \rightarrow Q$	$\neg(P \rightarrow Q)$
T	T	T	F
F	T	T	F
T	F	F	T
F	F	T	F

(b)

P	Q	$\neg Q$	$(P \wedge \neg Q)$
T	T	F	F
F	T	F	F
T	F	T	T
F	F	T	F

(c)

P	$P \wedge P$
T	T
F	F

(d)

P	Q	$\neg Q$	$P \rightarrow \neg Q$	$\neg(P \rightarrow \neg Q)$
T	T	F	F	T
F	T	F	T	F
T	F	T	T	F
F	F	T	T	F

(e)

P	Q	$\neg P$	$\neg P \to Q$
T	T	F	T
F	T	T	T
T	F	F	T
F	F	T	F

(f)

P	Q	R	$P \vee Q$	$P \vee R$	$(P \vee Q) \wedge (P \vee R)$
T	T	T	T	T	T
F	T	T	T	T	T
T	F	T	T	T	T
F	F	T	F	T	F
T	T	F	T	T	T
F	T	F	T	F	F
T	F	F	T	T	T
F	F	F	F	F	F

(g)

P	Q	R	$P \to Q$	$(P \to Q) \to R$
T	T	T	T	T
F	T	T	T	T
T	F	T	F	T
F	F	T	T	T
T	T	F	T	F
F	T	F	T	F
T	F	F	F	T
F	F	F	T	F

(h)

P	Q	R	$P \vee R$	$P \to (P \vee R)$
T	T	T	T	T
F	T	T	T	T
T	F	T	T	T
F	F	T	T	T
T	T	F	T	T
F	T	F	F	T
T	F	F	T	T
F	F	F	F	T

4 (a)

P	Q	R	$Q \land R$	$P \lor (Q \land R)$	$P \lor Q$	$P \lor R$	$(P \lor Q) \land (P \lor R)$
T	T	T	T	T	T	T	T
F	T	T	T	T	T	T	T
T	F	T	F	T	T	T	T
F	F	T	F	F	F	T	F
T	T	F	F	T	T	T	T
F	T	F	F	F	T	F	F
T	F	F	F	T	T	T	T
F	F	F	F	F	F	F	F

(b)

P	Q	$P \land Q$	$\neg P$	$\neg Q$	$\neg P \lor \neg Q$	$\neg(\neg P \lor \neg Q)$
T	T	T	F	F	F	T
F	T	F	T	F	T	F
T	F	F	F	T	T	F
F	F	F	T	T	T	F

(c)

P	Q	$P \land Q$	$\neg Q$	$P \to \neg Q$	$\neg(P \to \neg Q)$
T	T	T	F	F	T
F	T	F	F	T	F
T	F	F	T	T	F
F	F	F	T	T	F

5 (a) $A \land B$
 (b) $A \to B$
 (c) $(A \land B) \to C$
 (d) $A \to B$

6 (a) Either John drinks tea or he does not
 (b) If John drinks tea then John drinks milk
 (c) If John drinks either tea or coffee then John drinks milk
 (d) If John drinks tea then John does not drink coffee

7

P	Q	R	1 $\neg\neg P$	2 $P \to Q$	3 $P \land Q \to R$	4 $1 \land 2 \land 3$	5 $4 \to R$
T	T	T	T	T	T	T	T
F	T	T	F	T	T	F	T
T	F	T	T	F	T	F	T
F	F	T	F	T	T	F	T
T	T	F	T	T	F	F	T
F	T	F	F	T	T	F	T
T	F	F	T	F	T	F	T
F	F	F	F	T	T	F	T

8

P	Q	R	1 $P \vee Q$	2 $P \vee Q \to R$	3 $R \to P$	4 $Q \wedge 2 \wedge 3$	5 $4 \to P$
T	T	T	T	T	T	T	T
F	T	T	T	T	F	F	T
T	F	T	T	T	T	F	T
F	F	T	F	T	F	F	T
T	T	F	T	F	T	F	T
F	T	F	T	F	T	F	T
T	F	F	T	F	T	F	T
F	F	F	F	T	T	F	T

9

1. $\neg \neg P$	assumption
2. P	1 and double negation
3. $P \to Q$	assumption
4. Q	2, 3 modus-ponens
5. $P \wedge Q$	2, 4 $\wedge$ introduction
6. $P \wedge Q \to R$	assumption
7. R	5, 6 modus-ponens

10

1. Q	assumption
2. $P \vee Q$	1 $\vee$ introduction
3. $P \vee Q \to R$	assumption
4. R	2, 3 modus-ponens
5. $R \to P$	assumption
6. P	4, 5 modus-ponens

11.

P: David takes the maths lecture
Q: Class finishes early
R: David can get to the match

$P \to Q$
$Q \to R$
$\dfrac{P}{R}$

1. P	assumption
2. $P \to Q$	assumption
3. Q	1, 2 modus-ponens
4. $Q \to R$	assumption
5. R	3, 4, modus-ponens

Chapter 2

1 (a) True   (b) True   (c) True   (d) False   (e) False   (d) True

2 (a) True   (b) True   (c) True   (d) False   (e) True

3 (a) $\{-1, 0, 1, 2, 3\}$
   (b) $\{0, 1, 2, 3, 4, 5, 6, 7, 8, 9\}$
   (c) $\{6, 7, 9\}$
   (d) $\{Paris\}$

4 (a) 3   (b) 4   (c) 2   (d) 3

5 (a) $\{\{\}, \{2\}\}$
   (b) $\{\{\}, \{10\}, \{11\}, \{18\}, \{10, 11\}, \{10, 18\}, \{11, 18\}, \{10, 11, 18\}\}$
   (c) $\{\{\}, \{\{2\}\}, \{\{ \}\}, \{\{\}, \{2\}\}\}$

6 (a) $\{3, 4, 5, 8, 9, 11\}$
   (b) $\{3, 4, 5, 8, 9\}$
   (c) $\{9\}$
   (e) $\{blue\}$
   (f) $\{3\}$
   (g) $\{3\}$

7 (a) $\{5, 10\}$
   (b) $\{-12, -16, 12\}$
   (c) $\{8, 14\}$
   (d) $\{\}$
   (e) $\{-15, -14, 8, 14, 20\}$
   (f) $\{-16, -15, -14, -12, 12, 20\}$

8 (a) $\{(3, 6), (3, 8), (3, 2), (4, 6), (4, 8), (4, 2)\}$
   (b) $\{(6, 3), (6, 4), (8, 3), (8, 4), (2, 3), (2, 4)\}$
   (c) $\{(3, 3), (3, 4), (4, 3), (4, 4)\}$

Chapter 3

1 (a) True   (b) True   (c) True   (d) True   (e) False

2 (a) $\exists x.[\text{dog}(x) \wedge \text{eat}(x, \text{meat})]$
   (b) $\forall x.[\text{dog}(x) \rightarrow \text{eat}(x, \text{meat})]$
   (c) $\neg\exists x.[\text{dog}(x) \wedge \text{cat}(x)]$
   (d) $\exists x.[\text{dog}(x) \wedge \text{beautiful}(x)]$
   (e) $\neg\exists x.[\text{cat}(x) \wedge \text{beautiful}(x)]$
   (f) $\forall x.\exists y[\text{dog}(x) \rightarrow [\text{cat}(y) \wedge \text{chase}(x, y)]]$

3 (a) Nothing is both a dog and a cat
   (b) All beautiful dogs eat meat
   (c) Only dogs chase cats
   (d) Only dogs eat meat

Chapter 4

1 (a) transitive, antisymmetric   (b) transitive, antisymmetric, reflexive

2 (a) symmetric   (b) transitive, antisymmetric   (c) transitive, symmetric
   (d) transitive, symmetric, reflexive

3 transitive, symmetric, reflexive

4 ({Jane, Sara} × {Jane, Sara}) ∪ ({Dave, Peter, John} × {Dave, Peter, John})

5 domain = {1, 2, −1, −2} codomain = {1, 8, −1, −8}

6 {(3, 9), (4, 16), (5, 25), (6, 36), (7, 49)}

7 (a) function   (b) function   (c) not a function

8 (a) one–one   (b) onto   (c) one–one, onto, bijective   (d) one–one
   (e) one–one

9 $f^{-1}:\mathsf{N} \to \mathsf{N}$ $f^{-1}(x) = (x - 2)/4$

10 (a) 28   (b) 26   (c) 66   (d) $8x + 4$

Chapter 5

1 (a) $[4 \quad 3]$
   (b) $[4 \quad 3]$
   (c) $[-2 \quad 7]$
   (d) $[8 \quad -4 \quad 4]$
   (e) $[4 \quad -2 \quad -2]$
   (f) $[6 \quad -4]$
   (g) $[-6 \quad 4]$
   (h) $[4 \quad -2 \quad 6]$
   (i) $\sqrt{13}$
   (j) $\sqrt{14}$
   (k) -7
   (l) 18
   (m) $\begin{bmatrix} 2 \\ -1 \\ 3 \end{bmatrix}$

2 (a) -5
   (b) $\begin{bmatrix} 2 & 4 \\ 8 & -10 \end{bmatrix}$
   (c) $\begin{bmatrix} 5 & -2 & 4 \\ -6 & -21 & -10 \end{bmatrix}$

(d) $\begin{bmatrix} 1 & 2 \\ -4 & 1 \\ 0 & 2 \end{bmatrix}$

(e) $\begin{bmatrix} 5 & -6 \\ -6 & 41 \end{bmatrix}$

3 (a) -3

(b) $\begin{bmatrix} 8 & 12 & 6 \\ 4 & -6 & -4 \end{bmatrix}$

(c) $\begin{bmatrix} 28 & 22 & 45 \\ -11 & -8 & -11 \end{bmatrix}$

(d) $\begin{bmatrix} 1 & 3 & 2 \\ 1 & 2 & 2 \\ 3 & 5 & 1 \end{bmatrix}$

(e) $\begin{bmatrix} 61 & -16 \\ -16 & 17 \end{bmatrix}$

4 $x_1 = 2, x_2 = 2$

5 $x_1 = -1, x_2 = 3$

6 $x_1 = 1, x_2 = 1, x_3 = 2$

7 $x_1 = -2, x_2 = 1, x_3 = 3$

8 $x_1 = 3, x_2 = -1, x_3 = -1$

Chapter 6

1 8 and -5

2 $\begin{vmatrix} -3 & -1 \\ 0 & 3 \end{vmatrix}, \begin{vmatrix} 4 & 1 \\ 0 & 3 \end{vmatrix}$ and $\begin{vmatrix} 4 & 1 \\ -3 & -1 \end{vmatrix}$ the determinant is -34.

3 (a) -104 (b) 12   (c) 18   (d) 2

4 -60

5 -45

6 $\begin{bmatrix} 0.8 & -0.6 \\ -0.1 & 0.2 \end{bmatrix}$

7 $\begin{bmatrix} -0.58 & 0.6 & -0.24 \\ 0.38 & -0.2 & 0.04 \\ 0.27 & -0.2 & 0.27 \end{bmatrix}$

Chapter 7

1 (a) 3, 2

(b)
$$\begin{bmatrix} 0 & 1 & 0 & 0 & 1 & 0 \\ 0 & 0 & 1 & 1 & 0 & 0 \\ 0 & 1 & 0 & 1 & 0 & 0 \\ 0 & 1 & 1 & 0 & 0 & 1 \\ 1 & 0 & 0 & 0 & 0 & 1 \\ 0 & 0 & 0 & 1 & 1 & 0 \end{bmatrix}$$

(c)
$$\begin{bmatrix} 2 & 0 & 1 & 1 & 0 & 1 \\ 0 & 3 & 1 & 1 & 1 & 1 \\ 1 & 1 & 2 & 1 & 0 & 1 \\ 1 & 1 & 1 & 3 & 1 & 0 \\ 0 & 1 & 0 & 1 & 2 & 0 \\ 1 & 1 & 1 & 0 & 0 & 2 \end{bmatrix}$$

(d)
$$\begin{bmatrix} 0 & 4 & 1 & 2 & 3 & 1 \\ 4 & 2 & 4 & 5 & 1 & 2 \\ 1 & 4 & 2 & 4 & 2 & 1 \\ 2 & 5 & 4 & 2 & 1 & 4 \\ 3 & 1 & 2 & 1 & 0 & 3 \\ 1 & 2 & 1 & 4 & 3 & 0 \end{bmatrix}$$

2 Yes

3 5-1-2-3-4-6-5

4 Yes

5 A solution is 2-1-3-2-4-5-6-4-3

6 A solution is 3-1-4-5-3-2-1

7 (a) 6   (b) 2   (c) 6

8 ((j ((n o) m)) i)

9 6

10 a b e f c d g h i

11 e f b c g i h d a

12 a b d h j k l n o m i e c f g

13 j n o l m k h i d e b f g c a

14 Edges to include weights 10, 20, 40, 50, 60, 70

15 A sample is 10, 50, 60, 70, 80, 100

16 Edges to include 10, 20, 30, 40, 70

Chapter 8

1   $6 + 10 + 6$

2   $8 \times 4 \times 3$

3   2^6

4   $5 \times 4 \times 3 \times 2 \times 1$

5   216

6   120

7   105

8   132

9   126

10 $(3 \times 4) + (4 \times 6)$

11 $3 + 9 + 27$

12 15

13 1/6

14 1/32

15 21/36

16 1/336

17 $\dfrac{1}{10^5}$

18 2/3

19 1/7

20 1/11

Bibliography

Some further texts are recommended here. Some of the texts are specialist texts on the material introduced in this book and so they go into much greater depth. The other texts provide an introduction to fuzzy logic and neural networks.

There are two books that go into more depth with the subjects covered in this book and both books are highly recommended:

Judith Gersting, *Mathematical Structures for Computer Science,* second edition. W. H. Freeman and Company 1987.

Kenneth Ross and Charles Wright, *Discrete Mathematics,* third edition. Prentice Hall 1992.

An excellent book on logic is the book by Dov Gabbay.

Dov Gabbay, *Elementary Logics: A procedural perspective.* Prentice Hall Europe 1998.

An easy to read book with little mathematics is the introduction to fuzzy logic by one of the subject's influential figures, Bart Kosko.

Bart Kosko, *Fuzzy Thinking, The new science of fuzzy logic.* HarperCollins 1994.

For an introduction to neural networks

Robert Callan, *The Essence of Neural Networks.* Prentice Hall 1998

Introduces the subject with minimal mathematics and numerous examples to explain any complicated calculation. The book includes a chapter on introductory material to artificial intelligence in preparation for the final chapter that explores the emerging synthesis of traditional artificial intelligence techniques with those of neural networks.

A good text on linear algebra is

Fraleigh and Beauregard, *Linear Algebra,* third edition. Addison Wesley 1995.

Index